Why on Earth Do I Feel This Way?

Understanding Anxiety and Mental Health through Control Theory

REVISED EDITION

Why on Earth Do I Feel This Way?

Understanding Anxiety and Mental Health through Control Theory

REVISED EDITION

Jolene Arasz, Psy.D.

SYNOPSIS

Why on Earth Do I Feel This Way? brings an entirely new perspective to the field of anxiety and mental health and will make a drastic impact that no other treatment intervention has done before. As a psychologist who has worked in various clinical venues, I found there to be a pattern of anxiety at the root of the symptoms my clients were experiencing. This was the same pattern for clients who were battling addiction and experiencing mood disorders, schizophrenia, and even personality disorders. Although each case was unique, I would hear the same questions repeated: "Why me? Why on earth do I feel this way?" I stopped focusing on the specific symptoms of my clients that would qualify them for a mental health diagnosis but focused on how and why they were experiencing anxiety. I was then able to recognize another factor that was precipitating the anxiety: a lack of control.

Focusing on control, or lack thereof, as presented by control theory in the book, can supplement the work that people have been doing to manage their mental health and better help them understand why they have been making progress in their work. It will also provide a preventive approach to managing anxiety and mental health moving forward and increasing self-esteem and self-confidence by understanding what anxiety is, where it comes from, and what to do with it.

The information provided in this book can be utilized by various demographics, including adolescents, adults, parents (parents can also apply these tools for younger-age children), teachers, and other school personnel. There is a lack of preventive measures in place to help address anxiety at the forefront and prevent it from progressing into more severe mental health disorders or prevent students from engaging in maladaptive, harmful, and risky behaviors. Although schools have started taking additional steps to address mental health, they are still struggling to keep up with the need for services and are only targeting students who are at risk or suffering. Why on Earth Do I Feel This Way? provides students, parents, and teachers with a road map of how to effectively manage and get control over their anxiety.

ISBN: 978-1-957776-77-4 (Paperback)
ISBN: 978-1-957776-78-1 (Hardback)
ISBN: 978-1-957776-76-7 (Ebook)

Any references to historical events, real people, or real places are used
fictitiously.

GroveHouse Press LLC
340 S Lemon Ave #3529
Walnut, CA 91789
United States
www.grovehousepress.com

Contents

Disclaimer: This book is for educational purposes. It is not to replace or substitute any treatment by a doctor or other mental health care provider.

To be yourself in a world that is constantly trying to make you something else is the greatest accomplishment.

—Ralph Waldo Emerson

Introduction

On a summer afternoon, a mother brought her nineteen-year-old son to my office, complaining of him always being angry and yelling at her. Her son was silent throughout much of the session, slouched back in the chair, arms crossed, looking at the floor, and rolling his eyes every time his mother spoke. I obviously knew he did not want to be in my office. I was the third therapist to whom his mother had brought him. According to him, therapy was pointless. He's never benefited from it before and assumed I was going to be the same as every other therapist with whom he's worked. He didn't see any point in being there. As his mother continued to talk and describe his behavior, and not in the most supportive way, the dynamic between them materialized. I had to interrupt their exchange of words and started to describe my treatment approach. I didn't ask the son any questions during the intake. I knew he was not interested in talking, and I wasn't going to push him in our first meeting. However, I was hoping he would listen to what I had to say.

I described how my focus with my clients is anxiety based. I explained that every single person has anxiety, but it looks different from one person to the next. I described what anxiety is and that it is actually rooted in feeling a lack of control. When we don't have the level of control we need or want, our anxiety automatically intensifies. When the anxiety increases, that is where we see the behaviors. Every single one of us reacts to anxiety in our own way, whether it's something big or something small. That's what hooked him. His head popped up when I described the way in which control, or lack thereof, is at the root of our anxiety. I normalized it. I also caught the mother's attention. I then explained to him what we would work on to tackle that anxiety and put the control back into his hands. My client continued to come back to therapy every week until he went back to college, and by that time, he felt a whole other level of control that he never knew he could have.

Why on Earth Do I Feel This Way? aims to provide a basic understanding of anxiety and its impact on our daily lives. I'm writing this in hopes that I can raise awareness about and normalize anxiety and mental health. As a psychologist, my primary focus is helping my clients understand, become more aware of, and get control of their anxiety. *Control Theory* addresses just that. Anxiety is ubiquitous, underrecognized, and undertreated under the current paradigms. Control Theory offers a way to look at anxiety differently, to recognize its many forms, and to focus on certain aspects of anxiety that people can identify and gain control over.

The reason I feel it is so important for us to understand anxiety is that anxiety is at the root of everything with which we deal on a daily basis. The topic of anxiety is such an important topic for me. Through years of practice, I have found that anxiety is severely misunderstood, yet every single person experiences it. The problem is that most people are not necessarily aware that they are experiencing anxiety on a daily basis and easily misinterpret what they experience on a physical, mental, and emotional level. Anxiety also serves an important purpose; however, when people talk about anxiety, it's never addressed as a helpful mechanism, but how it's impeding a person's functioning.

Since the first edition of this book, I have been focusing much more on the neurobiology of anxiety trauma than what I presented in the first edition. I will still include information from the first edition; however, I will be providing a much more in-depth description of what is happening in the brain, not only when experiencing anxiety, but how trauma impacts the functioning of the brain, and how the neurobiology of anxiety and trauma go hand in hand with Control Theory. I will also include exercises to help re-regulate specific structures of the brain after having experienced prolonged anxiety or trauma. These will which also serve as protective measures to help strengthen structures of the brain to build resilience before experiencing anxiety or trauma, aiding in the brain to recover more quickly and effectively from potential anxiety or trauma.

In addition, I have expanded my practice of this work into various settings and with a vast range of clientele since the first edition of this book, including schools, colleges, and law enforcement. I will present what that work entailed, how it was received and utilized, and how I aim to continue to build on this work.

As stated in my previous book, I hope to provide my readers with a better (or more accurate) understanding of anxiety, appropriately and effectively control their anxiety from a cognitive and neurological approach. I want my readers to walk away from this book having a more in-depth understanding of where in the world anxiety comes from, as well as help decrease or prevent the use of maladaptive behaviors as a way to alleviate anxiety in a given moment.

The information provided in this book on anxiety, trauma, and Control Theory can be utilized by various demographics. The objectives can be used by adolescents, adults, parents (and parents applying these tools for younger-age children), teachers, coaches, and other school personnel. My ultimate vision is that mental health education be a requisite for schools and should be integrated as part of the mainstream curriculum, just as science, history, math, English, and other languages are. Until then, if we can start to implement these strategies in our schools, whether it be in elementary, middle school, high school, or even college settings, we can help students understand their anxiety in a way that helps facilitate the following areas: improving academic performance, stabilizing social relationships, prioritizing their individual needs and focusing on themselves in a healthy way, improving communication and interpersonal skills, setting clear and appropriate boundaries with others as well as for themselves, and learning how to take accountability for their own choices and responsibilities and how to hold others accountable. Control Theory and the cognitive and neurological objectives presented in this book aim to not only help us understand anxiety and its causes, but also to help in preventing or decreasing maladaptive behaviors, such as drinking, substance use, self-injurious behaviors, and violence.

Lastly, violence and gun control have been discussed and debated at length throughout our country; however, there has not been a consistent approach to mediating these issues. Gun control will continue to be debated. Unfortunately, no matter what the law states, we will continue to see escalated violence unless we get to the root of the matter. If it's not from a gun, it will be from something else. Violence is something we can work toward decreasing. In order to do this, we need to learn what causes us to think about and engage in such behaviors. If we can understand what is precipitating these thoughts, we can learn healthier, more appropriate ways to exercise control, rather than resorting to aggressive and violent behaviors. With this in mind, my work has also expanded to training law enforcement officers, about the neurobiology of the brain. This is to better understand how and why we react in high stress situations the way we do, and to better understand how to read another person with regard to their nervous system reactivity and know how to better engage with citizens versus reacting to the situation at hand based on misinterpreting the intentions and reactions of their citizens.

The vision of this book is to better equip students, caretakers, and communities to take on the challenges of modern society's stressors. Grounded in the proven methods of Cognitive Behavioral Theory and the most up to date neuroscience in the field of mental health, Control Theory will help people of all ages learn how to exercise control in healthy and appropriate ways in all aspects of their lives, thus helping prevent more severe symptoms or other potential mental health disorders, as well as preventing or decreasing maladaptive behaviors. We are working to build resilience in the brain to help us navigate ongoing and future stressors or, in a sense, to inoculate the brain. We can all have a healthy level of control in our lives, but we need to put some effort into learning about our anxiety and take accountability for our choices and actions. We have the power to gain healthy control, and when we do, we can make a big difference not only for ourselves but also in the world around us. This theory can be applied for all ages.

Part I: Anxiety Background

How Has Anxiety Traditionally Been Defined?

In order to understand what anxiety is, particularly through Control Theory, we first need to understand how anxiety is currently defined. According to the *Diagnostic and Statistical Manual of Mental Disorders, Fifth Edition* (*DSM-5*) (American Psychiatric Association, 2013), anxiety is defined as an *anticipation of a future threat*. Fear is also a component of anxiety, where the *DSM-5* defines fear as the *emotional response to a real or perceived imminent threat*.

The *DSM-5* presents several differential diagnoses of anxiety disorders, including generalized anxiety disorder, social anxiety, phobias, separation anxiety, selective mutism, and panic disorder. There is not much differentiation among these anxiety disorders, other than the actual object or circumstance that triggers anxiety. In order for anxiety to reach a clinical, diagnosable level, the *DSM* states that a person's daily functioning has been compromised (based on their set of symptoms) for a certain period of time (depending on age), and the anxiety is not attributed to the physiological effects of a substance or medication or due to another medical condition and is not better explained by another mental disorder. Here is where Control Theory takes a different approach. As we get into Control Theory, we will not just be focusing on anxiety as it reaches the level of becoming a "disorder"; rather, we will be looking at how typical a role anxiety plays in our day-to-day lives that is often overlooked or unrecognized. Control Theory can be applied even when we aren't experiencing extremely high levels of anxiety for basic anxiety that we might experience on a daily basis. Unfortunately, anxiety can be ubiquitous and misunderstood, which makes us vulnerable to not recognizing or appropriately treating our anxiety. Control Theory has a much broader approach to understanding anxiety and does not put as much emphasis on treating the specific symptoms that are manifested as a result of anxiety. It focuses on the underlying cause and provides an educational approach to helping people understand why they are feeling anxious in the first place.

Conventional Treatments and Theories

There have been a few common theories and treatment approaches to help manage anxiety as well as other disorders. One of the most common and empirically supported treatment approaches is that of Cognitive Behavioral Therapy (CBT). Other treatment approaches that have been helpful for managing anxiety and trauma include mindfulness, Dialectic Behavioral Therapy (DBT), and Eye Movement Desensitization and Reprocessing (EMDR). Mindfulness focuses on feeling grounded in the present moment. DBT focuses on teaching emotional regulation or how to better manage or control your emotions, and EMDR focuses on alleviating stress resulting from trauma or disturbing life experiences. All these approaches are beneficial, and I use EMDR in my private practice as well, but even these approaches have a common theme that isn't outwardly addressed in the theoretical explanations. That theme is control. Control Theory can be utilized alongside these theoretical approaches to help people understand *why* each of these theories can be successful. Each approach has its own objectives and specific goals. However, if we break down the objectives and recognize the end goals, each theory provides tools to help people increase their own personal sense of control. Control Theory provides a more general overall picture of how our focus on control can be applied across various life experiences. Although my clinical practice is based on Control Theory, I do incorporate mindfulness into my practices, as well as EMDR when treating more severe anxiety or trauma. I will elaborate on the mechanisms behind mindfulness and EMDR as I describe the neurobiology of anxiety and trauma.

Although Control Theory has a different approach to understanding and managing anxiety than other, more conventional theories, much of the cognitive work I do is based on the teachings of Judith Beck, who uses Cognitive Theory, stemming from the work of Aaron Beck. Both Aaron and Judith Beck have been and continue to be highly regarded as being among the most prominent psychologists in the field of cognitive therapy. Aaron Beck developed cognitive therapy in the 1960s. Cognitive therapy aims to be "a structured, short-term, present-oriented psychotherapy for depression, directed toward solving current problems and modifying dysfunctional thinking and behavior" (Beck, 1964; Beck, 1995). Cognitive therapy is specifically focused on identifying dysfunctional thoughts and replacing these thoughts with alternative, positive thoughts. The cognitive model presents several principles that guide the focus of the work. Some of the cognitive principles include assessing one's thinking in the current moment, problematic behaviors that result from distorted thoughts, identifying precipitating factors that influence a person's thought process, and identifying developmental events that influence a person's thought process and thought patterns. Cognitive therapy is goal oriented and problem focused and aims to be educational and prevent relapse. Cognitive theory teaches people how to identify, evaluate, and respond to their dysfunctional thoughts (Beck, 1995).

There are many common objectives in Control Theory and Cognitive Theory (an evidence-based practice), including being present oriented (which is also a component in the neurological work I do), identifying precipitating factors to anxiety, and identifying the thoughts and beliefs that trigger anxiety and the behaviors that result from that anxiety. They also both explore a person's developmental history, which may be influencing the way in which they interpret information. Both theories are educational in nature and aim to be preventative approaches to managing mental health issues and to manage anxiety more effectively in the future.

Where Control Theory differs from Judith Beck's Cognitive Theory is that Beck focuses on the importance of distinguishing between emotions and thought analysis while Control Theory presents a much broader description of anxiety. Control Theory views any negative emotion as a symptom of anxiety and focuses on a lack of control as the stimulus for anxiety. For example, Beck states that feeling anxious is different than feeling sad. Control Theory views any negative emotion as a way in which anxiety is manifested. According to Control Theory, each emotion is unique but is also a way of communicating that something doesn't feel right, and the individual doesn't have the level of control they need in that moment. Cognitive Theory doesn't address control or lack thereof as being a cause for anxiety.

Another way to distinguish Control Theory from Cognitive Theory is that Control Theory identifies the underlying theme of beliefs or the root cause of anxiety that sets the stage for our anxiety as we continue through development and into adulthood (which is also addressed in how our neurobiology is conditioned throughout our development), while Cognitive Theory analyzes each belief independently. The main objective of Control Theory is to teach others to shift control back into their own hands, cognitively and neurologically, which decreases their anxiety and increases their overall personal sense of control over themselves and/or the circumstances that triggered anxiety for them.

Control Theory also differs from another psychological concept, *locus of control*. Locus of control refers to how a person views their self. An internal locus of control means someone feels their personal efforts and abilities are the reason they are successful. An external locus of control means that a person perceives their successes as being due to external factors or luck. According to this theory, those who have an external locus of control are less likely to put forth significant effort to achieve something. They view their success as depending on circumstances, almost feeling as though they have limited to no control over the outcome. A person with an internal locus of control is assumed to be more achievement driven. Control Theory, along with the neurological objectives done within our work, reconditions our brain to shift its focus from the anxiety provoking thoughts and negative neural networks (which I will explain when applying neurobiology to anxiety) to building more adaptive, functional networks, while desensitizing our anxious thoughts. This allows us to accept the things over which we don't have control. We are training our brain to re-work itself to gain a stronger sense of personal control.

Part II

New Practice: Control Theory

Breaking Down Control Theory

Driven by the course of my work over the past 20 years, I have been able to develop an alternative theory of how to understand anxiety, which I refer to as Control Theory. Control Theory is a new theoretical approach to understanding what anxiety is, where it originates, and provides ways in which we can manage anxiety by focusing on our personal sense of control. Control Theory is based on the notion that anxiety develops when we are experiencing a lack of personal control. The general understanding is that when we don't have the level of control that we need or want, our anxiety increases. It provides a more general understanding of anxiety and a thematic approach to applying Control Theory in all aspects of life.

Many theoretical approaches to managing mental health are based on symptoms that, together, present as a disorder and focus on the diagnosis or class of symptoms. Control Theory specifically focuses on anxiety and management thereof, as well as treating trauma, because anxiety is at the root of any mental health disorder. By tackling the root cause of a disorder or trauma and learning how to control the underlying anxiety, we are able to minimize, decrease, or prevent the development of more severe symptoms that may then be categorized as another mental health disorder or a medical disorder. We are also retraining the brain to help strengthen and re-regulate areas that are impacted by prolonged anxiety or trauma. Anxiety is ubiquitous, underrecognized, and undertreated under the current theoretical and treatment paradigms. Control theory offers a way to look at anxiety differently, to recognize its many forms, and to focus on certain aspects of anxiety that people can identify and gain control over.

What Is Anxiety According to Control Theory?

So how does Control Theory define anxiety? According to Control Theory, anxiety is triggered when we experience a lack of sense of control. This might seem like a broad and vague description of anxiety. It is. That's part of why Control Theory is unique. Control Theory uses *anxiety* as a very general term. It views anxiety as any uncomfortable feeling that we experience. This includes feeling sad, angry, irritable, nervous, scared, et cetera. Any uncomfortable feeling—that's anxiety. It's our body's natural way of saying, "Something isn't right, here! I don't feel like my normal self." It's that natural *fight, flight, freeze or fawn* response when we don't feel we have the level of control we need/want in a particular situation. You might be wondering, "How is sadness anxiety? If you think about a time when you have felt sad, did you feel like you had control over the circumstances that made you feel sad? Chances are you were feeling sad because a situation was not going in a way in which you chose and felt your control was limited in some capacity.

Although anxiety has primarily served as a survival mechanism for all species, it has evolved for humans in such a way that it no longer serves our best self-interest. Our problem-solving abilities and social-emotional functioning are compromised as a result. I will discuss in greater detail how these compromises are manifested later in the book.

Let's compare Control Theory's definition of anxiety to the description of anxiety in the *DSM-5*. As previously mentioned, the *DSM* emphasizes anxiety based on excessive fear, stating that "fear is the emotional response to a real or perceived imminent threat." Fear differs from anxiety, according to the *DSM*: "Anxiety is anticipation of future threat." The *DSM* also lists panic attacks as a fear response.

Now let's think about fear and anxiety coming from the perspective of Control Theory. When we think about experiencing or perceiving a threat, what happens to our sense of control? It drops. If we are feeling threatened, we are not going to feel like we have control over what is happening to us or around us. If we did feel we had a greater sense of control, then our anxiety wouldn't feel overwhelming, and we wouldn't feel so threatened. The common thread that shows up in every case of anxiety is not a fear response; it's really a lack of feeling in control. Even if fear is strictly an emotional response, as the *DSM* states, that fear is still triggered when we don't have the control we need in that moment. When we anticipate something that triggers our anxiety, again, we are feeling a lack of control if we are anticipating a negative event. Furthermore, the DSM labels for mental illness are not aligned with specific patterns of brain activation. They are simply based on symptom classification, and do not assess the root cause of the symptoms.

When we perceive or anticipate an imminent or future threat, we don't feel we have a strong sense of control. If we are feeling sad, angry, annoyed, et cetera then we are likely not feeling the level of control we would like; therefore our anxiety (negative feeling) becomes stronger. When something doesn't go the way we planned, we don't feel we have the level of control that we want or need. When we don't get what we want, we feel a loss of control, resulting in frustration, anger, irritability, et cetera. When we undergo any kind of change or transition, we don't always have the level of control that we want or with which we would feel comfortable because we can't predict how the events will transpire. If we knew exactly how our life transitions would play out or could predict how changes or events would transpire, knowing exactly what to expect, then we would experience a higher level of control, which would naturally keep our level of anxiety low.

These are only a few examples of how the lack of a sense of control triggers a higher level of anxiety. I will go into further detail of how anxiety and control (or lack thereof) are present in other critical areas of our lives. First, let's get a better understanding of what the anxiety scale represents.

How Do We Better Recognize Anxiety? Applying the Anxiety Scale

To make anxiety more tangible, I will be using a numerical scale as a reference throughout the reading to demonstrate ways in which anxiety plays a role in various areas of our lives. The higher we are on the scale, the lower our sense of control or ability to personally affect a given outcome in a particular situation or circumstance will be. The numerical scale ranges from 0 to 10, where 10 represents the most intense level of anxiety. When our anxiety is high, we are actually experiencing low levels of control. This is the focus of our work: control. As we learn about anxiety, I will be focusing on the ways in which anxiety is rooted in experiencing a lack of control.

Using the anxiety scale can help us gain a better sense of awareness of how our anxiety is affecting us from moment to moment. It provides a visual tool to help us gauge the level of intensity of anxiety in the moment. Again, when our sense of anxiety is higher on the scale, it is due to our low sense of control. Below is a brief description of what anxiety levels might feel like on the scale from 0 to 10:

Anxiety Scale

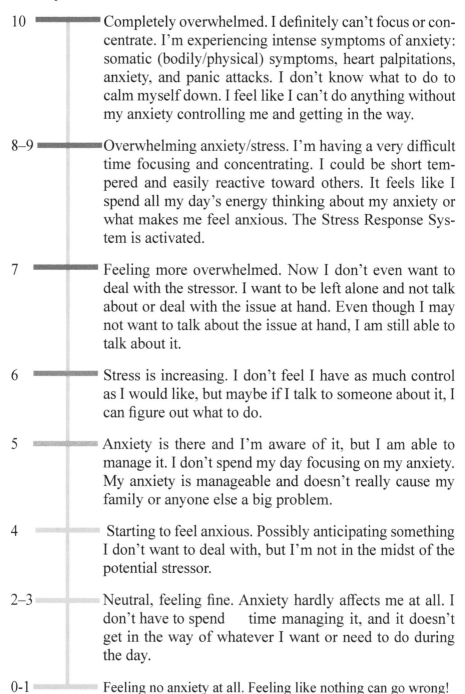

10 — Completely overwhelmed. I definitely can't focus or concentrate. I'm experiencing intense symptoms of anxiety: somatic (bodily/physical) symptoms, heart palpitations, anxiety, and panic attacks. I don't know what to do to calm myself down. I feel like I can't do anything without my anxiety controlling me and getting in the way.

8–9 — Overwhelming anxiety/stress. I'm having a very difficult time focusing and concentrating. I could be short tempered and easily reactive toward others. It feels like I spend all my day's energy thinking about my anxiety or what makes me feel anxious. The Stress Response System is activated.

7 — Feeling more overwhelmed. Now I don't even want to deal with the stressor. I want to be left alone and not talk about or deal with the issue at hand. Even though I may not want to talk about the issue at hand, I am still able to talk about it.

6 — Stress is increasing. I don't feel I have as much control as I would like, but maybe if I talk to someone about it, I can figure out what to do.

5 — Anxiety is there and I'm aware of it, but I am able to manage it. I don't spend my day focusing on my anxiety. My anxiety is manageable and doesn't really cause my family or anyone else a big problem.

4 — Starting to feel anxious. Possibly anticipating something I don't want to deal with, but I'm not in the midst of the potential stressor.

2–3 — Neutral, feeling fine. Anxiety hardly affects me at all. I don't have to spend   time managing it, and it doesn't get in the way of whatever I want or need to do during the day.

0-1 — Feeling no anxiety at all. Feeling like nothing can go wrong!

By applying the scale and giving ourselves a number we can identify when experiencing stress/anxiety, we are able to increase our emotional awareness. By using the scale, we can start to get a general understanding of our average level of anxiety on a daily basis. We become more aware of how much our anxiety might vacillate from day to day, or even throughout the day. We can start to see how our anxiety increases as our sense of control decreases. Our personal awareness of our anxiety increases. In order to work toward gaining control over our anxiety, we need to increase our sense of awareness regarding our uncomfortable emotions. We will continue to explore how our thought process plays a role in the fluctuation of our anxiety and control throughout the reading.

How Anxiety Can Be Manifested

Anxiety can be manifested in countless ways, including emotional dysregulation and physical or somatic (bodily) symptoms. Anxiety can be manifested emotionally (through anger, irritability, nervousness, sadness, and any other uncomfortable feeling); behaviorally (through impulsivity, aggression, shutting down, et cetera.); through somatic symptoms (headaches, shakiness, sweating, gastrointestinal problems, other physical ailments or illnesses); or through restlessness, feeling on edge, being fatigued, experiencing sleep disturbance, having difficulty concentrating or having one's mind going blank, muscle tension, worries, intrusive thoughts, et cetera.

It is very common for people who experience heightened levels of anxiety to develop gastrointestinal issues, including general abdominal pain, nausea, vomiting, irritable bowel syndrome (IBS), colitis, constipation, et cetera. Gastrointestinal problems are common in children and adults for a few reasons. First, the gut houses huge concentrations of nerves—almost as many as the brain. Our gut is actually considered to be our "second brain" because of how concentrated it is with nerves. These nerves react to stress just like our brain reacts. When these nerves are continuously reacting to stress, we are more prone to developing other symptoms in our gut. Second, when anxiety is triggered, our Sympathetic Nervous System (described below) is activated and prepares our body for fight, flight, or freeze. When this happens, blood rushes away from the stomach and intestinal tract to our muscles. As a result, we are not digesting whatever food is in our stomach. Eventually, the longer our body is in survival mode, food starts to ferment in the stomach, and there is a buildup of gas, creating acid reflux and other gastrointestinal issues. Third, as we remain in a heightened state of anxiety or frequently experience high levels of anxiety, the Stress Response System is continuously activated (I will discuss the Stress Response System in greater detail). There is a frequent or continuous release of cortisol that gets circulated through the intestinal track and back up to the brain. Cortisol itself is destructive to the intestinal walls, causing gastrointestinal issues.

In addition to a rush of blood going to our extremities, preparing our body to become as fast and strong as possible for fight or flight, blood also rushes to the brain. There is an intense rush of blood going through the small blood vessels in the brain, which can create intense pressure in the brain, causing headaches or migraines (Sweeten, 2019).

Anxiety can also be masked as different medical disorders and can present itself in numerous ways. A panic attack can often feel as though you are having a heart attack. Gastrointestinal issues also mask anxiety but are frequently diagnosed as other medical disorders. Autoimmune disorders result from the body's frequent and intense activation of the sympathetic nervous system and Stress Response System, where the body's immune system become overactive, resulting in inflammation (Maté, 2022). Although there are separate classifications of symptoms that make up a specific disorder, we need to look beyond strictly the visible symptoms. We need to pay close attention to our body's physical symptoms and functioning. As Dr. Bessel van der Kolk explains in his book, *The Body Keeps The Score*, the body responds to anxiety and trauma and holds on to that information until it is understood and resolved. Dr. Bessel Van Der Kolk and Dr. Gabor Maté discuss the in-depth levels at which our bodies are physically impacted by anxiety and trauma. Dr. Gabor Maté states that all our mental health afflictions and anxieties are in fact trauma, which is why I will be addressing the impact of not just anxiety, but trauma on the brain. By working through our traumas, we are working to self-actualize and become our real selves. In other words, we are working toward gaining a healthy, positive sense of control and self-agency.

The first thing we need to assess is a person's anxiety. When clients have previously been diagnosed with a disorder based on a handful of symptoms, I always start my work with them (after gathering background information and family and treatment history) by providing an educational approach to explain anxiety and then assess their own anxiety. When I focus on understanding their anxiety as well as where it's rooted, we can then move forward with utilizing clinical tools to manage their anxiety. As we gain more control over the anxiety, the symptoms that were providing diagnostic criteria for another disorder start to subside. It's not that these symptoms are not real (they are very real and can be excruciatingly painful, such as Fibromyalgia), but we need to look at the underlying causes of these disorders and not just take the symptoms at face value.

When a client experiences symptoms of various mental health disorders, including bipolar disorder, obsessive-compulsive disorders, or even symptoms of psychosis, these symptoms are oftentimes triggered when the client is under high stress/high anxiety, and their trauma neural networks are activated (which I will discuss further on in the reading). The symptoms are a reaction or a defense mechanism when the client is feeling so overwhelmed, they lose their personal sense of control. I've also had clients tell me that they never felt like they didn't have control, but after learning about what healthy control over their anxiety feels like, they recognize that the "control" they thought they had before was more of a false sense of control and their body's way of reacting to anxiety/stress in maladaptive ways, though they did not recognize this at the time.

It can be comforting for some people to continuously engage in compulsive behaviors, helping them feel like they have a sense of control over something in the moment, and that behavior and obsession help them avoid focusing on or dealing with the primary stressor. Psychotic symptoms, as well as dissociation, can also bring a sense of relief for people when they feel completely overwhelmed with what is happening in their life in the moment; they can "check out" when they are feeling highly overwhelmed, and it's too much to cognitively and emotionally process what they are experiencing in the moment. The brain and body have a way of automatically protecting us when experiencing anxiety and trauma, which is not a conscious choice that we make ourselves. (I will address what happens in the brain when dissociation occurs, including what purpose self-harm serves). I'm not trying to say that anxiety is the only cause of other disorders or symptoms such as psychosis, but these symptoms can be more easily triggered or escalated under stress or when anxiety is particularly high. Throughout my work, I have seen a consistent pattern when clients experience severe levels of anxiety. They are highly vulnerable to experiencing a wide range of symptoms.

When does anxiety become such a problem that it is considered to be a disorder? According to the *DSM-5*, anxiety becomes a disorder when it *persists beyond developmentally appropriate periods*. This means that the anxiety has been experienced for an extended period of time (typically six months or more according to the *DSM-5* diagnostic criteria, but it may be less for children). Although every single person has anxiety, and it is beneficial at appropriate times, it does not mean that everyone meets the clinical criteria for a disorder.

However, just because not everyone meets the diagnostic criteria for an anxiety disorder does not mean that we shouldn't pay attention to or understand our own anxiety or possible trauma history. In fact, if we learn more about our anxiety, pay more attention to the role it plays in our lives, and understand ways in which we can control it, we will be more likely to help prevent ourselves from reaching a diagnosable level of anxiety or other potential mental health issues. We will also be less likely to engage in maladaptive or unhealthy behaviors in a misguided effort to alleviate our anxiety. I will address how to use Control Theory as a preventative tool for maladaptive behaviors throughout the reading.

Although our anxiety can impede our functioning at times, it is very useful in certain situations and is a mechanism to keep us safe and alive. It can keep us vigilant when we are in dangerous situations, which is the primary purpose of anxiety. It's our warning signal when we are in danger or in an unsafe situation. Our brain is wired to keep us alive, and its default mode is to go into survival mode when our sense of safety is threatened. It can also motivate us to get things done or work hard to achieve something, such as a job promotion or school success. Healthy anxiety does indeed serve an important purpose, and we want to utilize this anxiety in healthy and productive ways. We also need to be able to recognize how our body is reacting when we start to experience anxiety. We can use physical experiences to help us recognize our anxiety and therefore focus on what is happening in the moment and engage in the cognitive work to help us manage the anxiety. However, when anxiety starts to interfere with our ability to focus on our priorities and affects our level of performance on a consistent basis, then we need to recognize the extent to which our anxiety has become unhealthy and is interfering with our daily lives. We want to utilize our anxiety to the degree that it is useful while also working to control it as best we can when it impedes our functioning. We also need to understand how the brain works when experiencing and managing anxiety and trauma. By understanding the structure and function of the brain, we can better understand the goals and objectives of therapy.

Understanding anxiety happens in many parts. We need to learn where our anxiety originates, what further triggers our anxiety, what it looks like for us independent of others, and ways in which we can control it so we can direct our focus where it needs to be, bringing our anxiety levels down and increasing our sense of control.

Part III

Where Anxiety Begins

Working Through the Body to Change the Brain

Although much of our work in managing anxiety is cognitive work, often times our anxiety or trauma is severe enough where we are not able to do the cognitive work yet. It is critical to understand how the body is not only impacted by anxiety and trauma, but how we use the body to treat anxiety and trauma. Much of my work, especially since the initial publication of this book, has been focusing on working through the body to change the brain. This is the key focus of trauma treatment providers, and stems from the research and work of Dr. Gabor Maté and Dr. van der Kolk. The goal of our work is to change the brain using the autonomic nervous system (ANS).

With every experience we have, our body and brain take in information via our senses, which travels through our spinal cord to our brain where the information is interpreted in a way that tells us if we are safe, unsafe, having a positive experience, uncomfortable experience, in control or out of control. Let us start by breaking down the nervous system and how it is organized.

The ANS consists of two branches – the sympathetic nervous system (SNS) and parasympathetic nervous systems (PNS). The ANS responds to stressful and threatening situations (when we experience a threat to or loss of personal control). The SNS prepares the body for fight or flight. It is the body's natural stress response. The PNS is the body's relaxation response to bring our nervous system back to its homeostasis, or resting state. Our brains are wired to be in this state of homeostasis most of the time (Sweeton, 2019).

The anxiety scale can be applied when gauging the sympathetic and parasympathetic nervous systems. As anxiety increases (going higher on the scale), the sympathetic nervous system (SNS) is activated. It prepares our body for fight or flight and to become faster and stronger when our safety is threatened (sensing a lack of control). Our brain and body are wired to recover from the short-term/temporary anxiety (coming back down on the scale), where the peripheral nervous system (PNS) is then activated to calm the body, bringing it back to its homeostasis. However, when we are faced with chronic, ongoing anxiety with minimal relief or recovery from stress or anxiety (when we are spending considerable time toward the top of the scale), our body and brain begin to experience other symptoms of anxiety, including depression, amongst other physical diseases or disorders. Furthermore, our brains can become traumatized from the prolonged anxiety, where specific structures that are involved in our emotional regulation and the SNS and PNS become dysregulated, weakened, and can malfunction (which I will explain in greater detail). Given today's social and political climate, this is where most of us are finding ourselves, and our daily functioning and relationships become compromised.

Although our brain can detect when we do not feel safe or have the level of control that we need, there are also physical indicators of anxiety that happen in our body when we experience high levels of anxiety or trauma. These physical reactions are supposed to serve a purpose and be aversive, telling us to get away from what is causing us distress (Sweeton, 2019). As previously mentioned, when the SNS is activated, blood exits the digestive system and goes to our muscles, preparing our body for fight or flight. Our muscles tense up and our body reacts to protect itself. Blood also rushes to our head but cannot go through the blood vessels all at once, creating a pounding headache. There is a loss of peripheral vision, creating tunnel vision. Eyes focus on what is threatening or the most salient aspect of the threat (Sweeton, 2019). It becomes problematic when we stay in the stress response (chronic stress or when we react to stress too strongly) for too long. According to Dr. Sweeton, there are over 1,400 biochemical and psychophysiological changes in the body when the SNS is activated (2019). Now think about where we are on the anxiety scale when the SNS is activated. As we go higher on the scale, our SNS is activated, and the stress response system (SRS) becomes activated as we get high enough on the scale (an 8 or above). Our brain is not wired for today's ongoing stressors, which is why prolonged anxiety compromises our functioning both physically and mentally. We want to be able to work through our body by using techniques to help us move from the stress response back to a relaxation response. I will present these techniques later in the reading.

Structure and Function of the Brain

As further evidence to show how anxiety affects our cognitive functioning and behaviors that I previously wrote about in the first edition, Dr. William Stixrud, neuropsychologist and coauthor of *The Self-Driven Child*, has presented a neuropsychological model of what is happening in the brain when we are experiencing different levels of anxiety. I will show how his neuropsychological model reinforces Control Theory. I will also be discussing research by Dr. Bessel van der Kolk to provide more context to the workings of the brain. To begin with, the National Scientific Council on the Developing Child identifies three types of stress:

1) Positive Stress:

This level of stress (anxiety) acts as a motivational factor for us to take the risks necessary to learn, grow, and work toward accomplishing short- or long-term goals. Applying Control Theory, an example of this level of stress might be when preparing for a test or competing at a sporting event. We might get nervous before the test or the event, but our anxiety can actually work to help us prepare ourselves as best we can by holding us accountable for studying or practicing our sport. (This is also where our anxiety can start to take too much control over us, where we can start to have thoughts or assumptions that we are going to fail or not perform well.) If our anxiety is not overwhelming or taking too much control over us and we are still able to maintain focus and concentration, we are going to be more likely to perform at an optimal level.

2) Tolerable Stress:

This level of stress (anxiety) occurs for relatively brief periods of time (not chronically), and we are able to recover from this temporary anxiety. An example of this type of stress when applying Control Theory might be experiencing a loss, such as a breakup, a friend moving away, or even a death. Experiencing loss lowers our sense of control as we are not choosing for these losses to happen, and they personally affect us. These events are out of our control and are often unexpected. It might take some time for us to process these losses as we experience different emotions about these events. However, as we continue to process these losses, we eventually work our way to a place of acceptance. We might still be sad that these events happened, but we are better able to live with these changes in our lives.

3) Toxic Stress:

This level of stress and anxiety is chronic, lasting for longer periods of time or happening more frequently, is more difficult to recover from, and is a prolonged activation of the neurological stress system. Here, we feel that such chronic stress is never-ending, or we do not see a way out. When applying Control Theory, this is when we have been experiencing a high level of anxiety for a prolonged period of time or have experienced a traumatic event (abuse, bullying, witnessing assault, being in an accident, etc.), and we feel we have (or have had for a period of time) zero control. We hit a wall, and we are not able to effectively process such stressors anymore. We are physically, mentally, and emotionally wiped out. We do not have the energy to care or the motivation to do things anymore, and we experience the onset of depression.

As we remain in a state of depression, we start to feel more helpless and hopeless about there being a way out of this state. We have tried anything and everything we can think of, but nothing works. As Dr. Stixrud addresses, this is the level of stress that kids and adolescents often experience today. They have a difficult time managing daily pressures, such as getting the best grades, being compared to their peers, making sure they do enough community service for their college applications, taking AP classes in high school to bring up their GPAs, taking SAT prep classes, applying to the top colleges, playing sports or an instrument, participating in extracurricular activities, and the list goes on. More and more people are seeking help for mental health—anxiety, depression, and suicides are still rising (van der Kolk, 2015). This brings us back to the importance and main objective of Control Theory: to help students (and everyone) focus on themselves and what is in their own best interests, rather than taking on the expectations of others, and to understand how to regulate and strengthen structures of the brain to help build resilience and recover from anxiety and trauma. As Dr. Stixrud indicates, this type of stress is debilitating for students and does not prepare them to manage their anxiety in the future. When students are focused on pleasing others, according to Control Theory, they are feeding their anxiety and not learning how to problem-solve.

As previously mentioned, not all anxiety is bad. We need a healthy level of anxiety to motivate us to work hard and be successful in different areas of our lives. Dr. Stixrud also emphasizes the importance of optimal anxiety. The healthy level of anxiety that Dr. Stixrud refers to is short term or intermittent, and we are able to recover from this anxiety/stress and use it in a way that helps us be productive, focus, concentrate, and perform at a more optimal level. This is when the PNS is activated and brings our nervous system back to its homeostasis or resting state, which is what our brain is wired to do, allowing us to recover from the anxiety. Simultaneously, our brain is being conditioned to accurately interpret what is happening in the moment versus misinterpreting the anxiety as being unsafe, and the frontal lobe stays online to work through the anxiety (I will discuss this further when addressing specific structures of the brain). Self-care is important in aiding our recovery from anxiety and helping maintain healthy functioning of the structures of the brain that are active under stress.

Before we get further into identifying the specific structures of the brain involved in anxiety and trauma, let us start with looking at the distinct roles of the right and left hemispheres.

Each hemisphere plays different yet integrated responsibilities of our cognitive and emotional functioning.

Left Hemisphere: Positive emotions

Approach behaviors

Labels thoughts and feelings

Practical language

Develops new narratives

Focused more on tasks

More active in detail monitoring

Right Hemisphere: Prosody (tone of voice)

Self-regulation

Empathy

Intuition

Negative emotions

Withdrawal behaviors

Attunement (connecting with others)

Awareness of body

Circuits of attachment

Each hemisphere is activated for different tasks or under specific circumstances; however, the right hemisphere was developed first as it is critical for survival and attachment (Sweeton, 2019). When our SRS is activated, it is our right hemisphere that is highly activated, and the left hemisphere is minimally activated (Sweeton, 2019). Compare this to Control Theory, as our anxiety increases and we go higher on the anxiety scale, particularly at an 8, 9, or 10. This is when the right hemisphere is highly activated. We are more in a reactive state where we are likely to engage in avoidance behaviors and react when we interpret others' body language and tone of voice to be negative. We can quickly assume or interpret how someone might be judging us or feel about us based on their body language and tone of voice, further increasing our anxiety, and engaging in more reactive or avoidant behaviors. Without the left hemisphere engaged to work with the right hemisphere, we will stay in a reactive state. We need the left hemisphere to activate and engage with the right hemisphere to slow or stop the stress response system (SRS) to then be able to do the cognitive work to manage our anxiety. I will address bilateral stimulation (activating both hemispheres) when discussing treatment recommendations.

As we experience a situation where our brain receives information that we are not safe, our sympathetic nervous system is activated, and the body prepares to defend itself against the stressor. However, there is another defense response in addition to fight or flight, which is a freeze response. This is when something traumatic happens and the body becomes immobilized. It can be a collapsing response, where the muscles go flaccid and you can lose consciousness, or it might be a mobility response, where the muscles get very stiff, and you can't move. You might not be able to talk. The body's SNS is activated for flight or flight; however, both the SNS and PNS are activated during the freeze response (Sweeton, 2019). Ideally, we want to have a balance within the ANS, where we are not completely consumed by either SNS or PNS, as displayed in the graph below:

Sympathetic Nervous System (SNS) activation – Fight or Flight

Social engagement (we want to be here)

Parasympathetic Nervous System (PNS) activation – activated to create the freeze response; dissociation; brain and body disconnect (Sweeton, 2019).

When we are experiencing high anxiety or traumatic events, we do not get to choose which defense mode our body engages (Sweeton, 2019). Children and adolescents often freeze, as well as victims of sexual violence. It is supposed to be an adaptive survival response. The brain quickly assesses the situation to determine what defense response would have the greatest rate of survival. This happens outside of conscious awareness and outside of conscious control. Freezing can be very adaptive. Once the body freezes, and survives the trauma, it is likely to freeze again as it has previously kept you alive (Sweeton, 2019). When you freeze, your body does not move and does not get rid of the traumatic energy, compared to if we engage in fight or flight, the body moves and communicates with the brain that the trauma is over, and the nervous system rebalances. Exercise promotes a shaking movement of the brain and helps the body's memory of the trauma get resolved and rebalance the nervous system (Sweeton, 2019).

Key Structures of the Brain Involved in Anxiety and Trauma

In the first edition of Why On Earth Do I Feel This Way, I presented some information on what is happening in the brain when we experience anxiety and depression. However, my focus was more on the chemical reactions happening in the brain versus presenting a more thorough picture of the critical structures and their functions that play a significant role in helping us manage or regulate anxiety, and how these structures are impacted by chronic anxiety and trauma. I will be building on the information of what I presented in the first edition.

The goal of our work here is to better understand how five specific structures of the brain are negatively affected by anxiety, prolonged anxiety, and trauma, and to learn what we can do to help repair, strengthen, and re-regulate these structures. By practicing specific brain-based and body- based techniques, we are increasing our self-awareness and training our brain to regulate structures of the brain to prevent us from potentially becoming traumatized if we do in fact experience trauma or chronic anxiety. In other words, we are training our brains to be resilient against future trauma and anxiety. The brain and body are built to regulate itself naturally. We need to make sure we teach ourselves to regulate our nervous system. The nervous system becomes dysregulated when experiencing chronic anxiety and trauma. The following information on the specific brain structures is referenced from Dr. Jennifer Sweeton's trauma treatment resources. I will first present the key structures that are involved in anxiety and emotion regulation, and then present how the stress response system is activated and what happens during that process.

Thalamus

The thalamus is the initial point of entry, or relay station, where information enters our brain through our senses (sight, touch, taste, hearing), excluding smell. Information comes to the thalamus, which then sends information to the amygdala and/or the prefrontal cortex (Sweeton, 2019). Information we receive from smell goes directly to the amygdala.

Amygdala

The amygdala is considered the brain's fear center. The job of the amygdala is to determine whether a particular situation, person, context, etc., presents a threat or danger (Sweeton, 2019). I have always referred to the amygdala as the "fire alarm" in the brain that goes off after receiving information that we are not okay or not safe, and do not have an adequate sense of personal control. Dr. Bessel van der Kolk also refers to it as the "smoke alarm". When undergoing high anxiety or experiencing trauma, the amygdala is activated and triggers the Stress Response System (SRS) to prepare the brain for survival. It can become overly sensitive to information (and therefore overactive) the more we experience elevated levels of anxiety or trauma and are not able to regulate our sympathetic and parasympathetic nervous systems, particularly with Post Traumatic Stress Disorder (PTSD) (Sweeton, 2019). With PTSD, the amygdala can pick up information and interpret it as a threat even if there is no actual threat. The "perceived threat" causes the amygdala to suppress activation of the cortex (thinking brain).

Even though the amygdala becomes extremely sensitive due to the trauma, it also has its own internal system to determine what information is dangerous and what is not dangerous. It consults with the hippocampus (the memory center – described below) to determine if something is dangerous. The hippocampus constantly communicates to the amygdala, providing more context to help the amygdala determine if something is safe or not (Sweeton, 2019). The goal of our work is to calm the amygdala down or deactivate the stress response system that is activated by the amygdala. We can do this using various techniques, which I will address further in our work.

Insula

The insula is considered the interoception center. It has several jobs. It is responsible for both interoception (feeling into the body for internal sensations; sensing if the body is hot, cold, hungry, thirsty, etc.) and proprioception (sense of where our body is located in space and balance) (Sweeton, 2019). We need physical sensations to feel emotions. Another way to put it; emotions are physical sensations (van der Kolk, 2015; Maté, 2022; Sweeton, 2019). The insula also provides information to the amygdala of whether we are safe or not safe. It is a very primitive structure of the brain, like the amygdala, and provides information to the amygdala with minimal context. It can quickly and easily misinterpret information from our experiences as being unsafe as it does not assess other relevant information to form an accurate interpretation.

For example, if I've had a panic attack in a grocery store and return to the same store a month after having the panic attack, my insula may quickly interpret my experience as "I'm not safe. Get out". However, the insula does not take into account that there is nothing happening to me at that moment and that I'm actually safe. It will communicate to the amygdala that I'm not safe and to sound off the alarm.

The insula becomes dysregulated under trauma or severe anxiety. It can become overactive, or underactive. When underactive, you might experience more dissociative symptoms or numbing. When overactive, you may see more emotional reactivity or outbursts, or be extremely sensitive to changes in internal states (Sweeton, 2019). With trauma, the insula is underactive. We need to have sensations to have any interpretation or emotion. When someone is re-experiencing sensations, there is hyperactivity in the insula, leaving us experiencing the same feeling as when we were traumatized (van der Kolk, 2015; Maté, 2022; Sweeton, 2019). We need a healthy, balanced, and well-regulated insula to accurately interpret what we are experiencing. The goal of treatment is to strengthen the insula, so it becomes re-regulated. I will address treatment objectives to strengthen and re-regulate the insula further in the reading.

Hippocampus

The hippocampus is our memory center. As previously stated, it communicates closely with the amygdala. It is involved in learning and is also considered a "timekeeper" by Dr. Bessel van der Kolk (2015). The hippocampus is the memory center for explicit, autobiographical, and declarative information. It can recall information and communicate to us when events have transpired in our lives (van der Kolk, 2015; Stixrud & Johnson, 2018; Sweeton, 2019). It tells us that we experienced past events in the past, not in the present. The hippocampus is also interested in emotional information. If we have an emotional reaction to something, the more likely we will remember the event (Sweeton, 2019).

The presence of cortisol, which is released once the Stress Response System (SRS) is activated, is a significant factor in how accurate the hippocampus is able to code and form memories (van der Kolk, 2015; Sweeton, 2019). Cortisol can flood the hippocampus, which is covered in cortisol receptors, preventing the hippocampus from fully activating. For those who experienced trauma or chronic anxiety, the hippocampus functions at a slower rate due to neurons being damaged and killed off by cortisol (Stixrud & Johnson, 2018; Sweeton, 2019). Our focus and memories are fragmented when our hippocampus is flooded with cortisol, and we aren't able to discern the accurate order of memories. This is one reason why eye-witness testimony is controversial. The hippocampus is not able to regulate itself due to hyperactivity of the amygdala which damages the hippocampus and causes errors in memory and coding (van der Kolk, 2015; Stixrud & Johnson, 2018; Sweeton, 2019). The hippocampus can eventually start to atrophy and die. Triggers for anxiety can also happen when the hippocampus gives faulty information to the amygdala as a result of being damaged. We can prevent some triggers by training the hippocampus and consolidating memories (Stixrud & Johnson, 2018; Sweeton, 2019). I will address how we can train the hippocampus and undo damage done to the hippocampus by cortisol further in the reading.

Cingulate Cortex

The cingulate cortex, also known as the anterior cingulate cortex (ACC) is referred to as the self-regulation center. It is involved in behavior regulation, conflict monitoring, error detection, and self-regulation, including regulation of emotions and thoughts (Sweeton, 2019). The cingulate tells us if we've made a mistake. It catches when we lose focus. In other words, it helps us refocus our attention when our mind starts to wander. The cingulate works closely with the prefrontal cortex (PFC). Each time we catch our mind wandering and refocus on what we are doing in the moment, our cingulate is what allows us to catch our attention and refocus.

The cingulate becomes weakened and underactive after experiencing trauma or chronic anxiety, making it much more difficult for us to regulate our emotions and thoughts, decision-making, or judgment (Sweeton, 2019). However, the error detection center is too active with obsessive compulsive behaviors. The more we engage in the behaviors, the stronger it reinforces the error detection center. The goal of therapy is to strengthen the cingulate to help us regulate painful emotions and manage distressing thoughts. The stronger the cingulate, we are more adept to down-regulate activation of the amygdala, leading to less-emotional reactivity to trauma triggers (Sweeton, 2019).

Prefrontal Cortex (PFC)

The prefrontal cortex is considered to be the thinking part of our brain. It is made up of several smaller structures that together are considered the thinking center of the brain. The PFC is involved in much of our executive functioning, or higher order thinking such as focus, concentration, judgment, planning, organizing, decision-making, problem solving, self-awareness, social-emotional regulation, and awareness of others (van der Kolk, 2015; Stixrud & Johnson, 2018; Sweeton, 2019). In a traumatized or highly anxious brain, the PFC is underactive, making it difficult to focus, concentrate, or make sound decisions. We become more reactive to our environment when the PFC is not able to function the way it should. Our goal in treatment is to make the PFC more active, which increases our ability to focus, think more clearly, improve concentration, make decisions, connect with others, and have more self-awareness (Sweeton, 2019). I will address how the amygdala affects the PFC functioning when discussing the stress response sys-

The Brain on Trauma

UNDERACTIVE
Self-Regulation Center (Cingulate)

DYSREGULATED
Interoception Center (Insula)

UNDERACTIVE
Memory Center (Hippocampus)

UNDERACTIVE
Thinking Center (Prefrontal

OVERACTIVE
Fear Center (Amygdala)

tem. It is not a survival area of the brain but is where much of our mental health lies. As previously mentioned, the prefrontal cortex is still under development during adolescent years. It doesn't stop developing until 27 years of age, and our emotional regulation is not fully developed until our early thirties (van der Kolk, 2015; Stixrud, 2019; Sweeton, 2019).

Stress Response System: Connection between the brain and body

Now that we've identified the key structures of the brain involved in anxiety and trauma and the breakdown of the nervous system, let's walk through the sequence of events when the stress response system (SRS) is activated. When we experience an event, our brain is receiving information through our senses. As previously mentioned, the information we receive through sight, touch, taste, and sound, travels through the spinal cord up to the brain for processing. Information enters our brain through the thalamus. Smell is the only sensory information that does not pass through the thalamus, but goes directly to the amygdala (Sweeton, 2019). This is why smells can be very intense and can easily trigger anxiety as well as happy or pleasant memories, otherwise experienced as nostalgia.

The thalamus can send information to two parts of the brain. The first area where information is sent from the thalamus is the prefrontal cortex (PFC). However, because the PFC is not closely located to the thalamus, it can take longer for information to travel from the thalamus to the PFC. The other area of the brain that receives information from the thalamus is the amygdala. The amygdala is located very close to the thalamus (Sweeton, 2019). You can think of them as next-door neighbors, whereas the PFC lives all the way across town from the thalamus. Information traveling from the thalamus to the amygdala is an extremely fast, short route, whereas information traveling from the thalamus to the PFC is very slow and is a much longer route. Given this, information that is interpreted as threatening is relayed very quickly to the amygdala, which is the activation site of the SRS. Remember that the amygdala acts like a fire alarm, and when it receives information that our safety (or control) is threatened, it sounds off the alarm, telling the hypothalamus to release dopamine and norepinephrine, and the SRS is activated. While this is happening, information is still traveling up to the PFC. Our brain is likely to have already activated the SRS before information gets to the PFC; therefore, we are less likely to be able to think our way through the situation or problem solve as far as what we need to do, let alone stay focused on what we are able to do in the moment.

Remember the PFC is the thinking part of our brain. However, when the amygdala is activated, the SRS starts to interfere with the functioning of the PFC. Depending on how strong the threat is that is communicated to and interpreted by the amygdala, the less we are able to access the PFC. Dr. Sweeton uses the example of a dial. When the threat is strong, the dial turns up, interfering more with the PFC. The amygdala essentially sends a message to the top of our brain, shutting down the PFC. That message can also interfere with the information that is traveling to the PFC from the thalamus, and can distort that information, so by the time the original information gets to the PFC, it's inaccurate information than what was initially interpreted from our experiences. This is another reason eyewitness testimony is controversial. They may be "remembering" inaccurate or distorted information than what had actually happened.

The frontal lobe also relies on two important neurotransmitters: dopamine and norepinephrine (Stixrud and Johnson, 2019). When we experience mild stress, arousal, or excitement, the levels of dopamine and norepinephrine increase just enough to where we can be more highly attuned to what we are doing in the moment. We are able to have clearer focus and concentration. However, when we experience higher levels of anxiety or chronic or prolonged anxiety, our ability to focus, concentrate, and problem-solve is compromised as the PFC becomes overloaded with dopamine and norepinephrine, which is when our SNS and SRS are activated (Stixrud & Johnson, 2019; Sweeton, 2019).

We become more reactive and defensive the stronger the activation of the amygdala, slowing or shutting down the PFC, and higher levels of dopamine and norepinephrine are released. An example of what this feels like is if you have ever been so overwhelmed, angry, or upset that you do or say something in the moment as a reaction, but later once you've settled down, you recognize and regret what you did or said. You might think to yourself, "I can't believe I did that". (It happens to every one of us!) That happens because your PFC was offline and was not able to stop you from doing or saying something that you knew you shouldn't have done but did it anyway.

This is consistent with Control Theory in that when we are at the top of the scale, we aren't necessarily aware of the fact that our anxiety is high and our sense of control is low, but we are highly aware that we don't like that feeling. If we are not necessarily aware of our anxiety or how we are interpreting information around us, and we don't like the way we are feeling but do not have proper tools to manage our anxiety and get back appropriate control, we are likely to engage in whatever is at our fingertips to help us feel better. This is oftentimes impulsive and maladaptive behavior. It is a natural defense mechanism to feel on guard or protect ourselves when we feel threatened or a loss of control. We are less likely to think clearly or to identify appropriate options that are within our control to manage the stressful situation. We might feel better in the moment when we engage in these impulsive or maladaptive behaviors, bringing a temporary sense of relief or a false sense of control. But our actual sense of control stays low as we are not managing the root cause of the problem. Our anxiety will quickly return to a higher level, oftentimes worse than it was before. By not engaging in the right exercises to train our brain and nervous system to become reregulated, we are preventing our brain from learning proper regulation. Therefore, we are increasing the sensitivity of the amygdala, weakening the PFC, hippocampus, and cingulate, and dysregulating the insula, making it harder for us to recover from anxiety and trauma. We also struggle to allow the PNS to help stabilize us.

Returning to the SRS, the amygdala also communicates to the hypothalamus which regulates the autonomic functions and activates the SRS, starts to shut down the PFC, and communicates to the pituitary gland. The Pituitary gland releases more chemical messengers that communicate with the adrenal glands to secrete cortisol. The cortisol works its way through the digestive tract and makes its way back up to the brain, attaching to the hippocampus as discussed earlier.

Here is a flow chart to present the chain of events when the Stress Response System (SRS) is activated. This is also referred to as the Hypothalamic Pituitary Adrenal (HPA) Axis.

Hypothalamic Pituitary Adrenal Axis (HPA Axis)
of the Stress Response System (SRS)

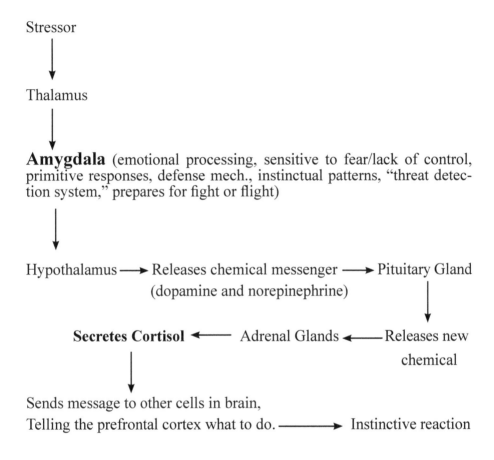

Stressor

Thalamus

Amygdala (emotional processing, sensitive to fear/lack of control, primitive responses, defense mech., instinctual patterns, "threat detection system," prepares for fight or flight)

Hypothalamus ⟶ Releases chemical messenger ⟶ Pituitary Gland
(dopamine and norepinephrine)

Secretes Cortisol ⟵ Adrenal Glands ⟵ Releases new chemical

Sends message to other cells in brain,
Telling the prefrontal cortex what to do. ⟶ Instinctive reaction

Once again, over time, if we are not able to recover from the anxiety or trauma in healthy ways or continue to experience severe anxiety for a prolonged period of time, our memory begins to be impaired. As discussed earlier, the hippocampus becomes underactive as cortisol floods the hippocampus. The neurons on the hippocampus start to die off, causing the hippocampus to atrophy and shrink, resulting in memory difficulties (Stixrud & Johnson, 2018; Sweeton, 2019). Memories stored while under high stress can be distorted, or not even stored at all in part due to the under activation of the hippocampus (Sweeton, 2019). Dr. Stixrud explains that this is why students often have a difficult time learning and retaining information when under stress. It is common for people who have experienced trauma or high anxiety for a prolonged period of time to have a smaller and less active hippocampus compared to others who have not experienced trauma or severe anxiety, or who have been able to manage their anxiety more healthily and effectively (Sweeton, 2019).

Because the hippocampus stores our memories, it can use these memories to help bring another frame of reference to our conscious awareness when we are experiencing a stressful situation. It provides more context to the situation, so the insula stays in check and accurately interprets what is happening in the moment. It helps us remember that we have had similar experiences before and were able to survive them or work through them, helping us calm down in the moment of high anxiety. For example, if I have a panic attack (for whatever reason) when I'm in a grocery store where I frequently shop, and the next time I enter the same grocery store, my insula can quickly react and misinterpret what I'm currently experiencing. My insula might automatically tell the amygdala, "We weren't safe here before. Get out! Get out! Get out!" The insula tries to tell the amygdala to sound off the alarm and activate the SRS. Meanwhile, my hippocampus kicks in and tells the insula to settle down as it provides more context to the situation. My hippocampus recognizes that, although I had a panic attack the last time I was in the store, I've also been in the same store numerous times before and I've been fine. I'm able to recognize that, at this current moment, nothing is happening and I'm safe. My hippocampus then communicates to the amygdala to NOT sound off the alarm because nothing bad is happening in the moment. Because my amygdala does not activate the SRS, my frontal lobe stays online and I'm able to come up with a plan for what I need to do in the moment. I can go into the store, get what I need and leave, maintaining a sense of control over the situation.

When someone experiences extreme levels of anxiety to the point where they become traumatized, their neurotransmitters are overloaded, the stress-response system is activated and cortisol is released, making it more difficult for the person to recover from the stress of the experience, thus damaging the hippocampus. If the hippocampus is damaged, the person is not able to recall useful information or memories of how to cope with stress. The hippocampus becomes vulnerable to taking "fuzzy" pictures of the event, making the experience of the event more open for interpretation. This leads to generalization of fear (van der Kolk, 2015; Sweeton, 2019). Without treatment, generalization gets worse, along with avoidance behaviors.

People with PTSD are not able to bring other perspectives to a new stressful situation that is in any way similar to a previous traumatic experience (Stixrud and Johnson, 2018). They are not able to accurately put their current experience into proper context or recognize that it is not the same situation. They are highly vulnerable to experiencing a level of anxiety like what they experienced during the traumatic event (van der Kolk, 2015). Furthermore, we might forget how long or when the trauma occurred. Memories don't age with trauma. Our bodies will react the same way when we think about the traumatic events as when we first experienced it (van der Kolk, 2015: Stixrud & Johnson, 2018; Sweeton, 2019). In other words, our brain is not able to recognize that the traumatic event happened in the past. It acts as if (and keeps reliving) the event is taking place in real time, making us feel we are constantly living in the trauma (van der Kolk, 2015; Sweeton, 2019).

So, while the hippocampus starts to atrophy due to chronic anxiety or trauma, the amygdala becomes more sensitive to fear, or anxiety-provoking information, after we experience chronic stress or trauma. The amygdala becomes enlarged when we have been experiencing chronic stress, making us more vulnerable to reacting or experiencing heightened anxiety more frequently (Stixrud & Johnson, 2018; van der Kolk, 2015; Sweeton, 2019). As the amygdala becomes enlarged, the PFC is compromised, the insula becomes dysregulated, causing us to easily misinterpret information and it becomes exceedingly difficult to distinguish between information that is actually threatening and information that is not, resulting in more generalized anxiety.

Remember that our brain is wired to react physically and mentally to threatening situations to keep us alive but is also wired to allow us to recover from the threatening, even traumatic situations once the event ends. Our PNS is supposed to activate once the event or trauma is over, allowing for us to return to our homeostasis, and for the nervous system to calm down and rebalance itself. Unfortunately, nowadays, we are experiencing situations or life circumstances that are highly stressful, and ongoing, leading to chronic anxiety and trauma. Our brains and bodies are not able to quickly (if at all) recover from the daily anxieties we are facing. We are living with excessive levels of anxiety, which is altering the structure and function of our brains. It is healthy to experience a quick, temporary increase in stress, as long as we are able to "recover" from it (Stixrud and Johnson, 2019; van der Kolk, 2015; Sweeton, 2019). This means that the hormones involved in the stress response are able to come back down, allowing us to experience relief. In Control Theory, this is also considered a healthy increase in stress. If we are able to experience anxiety and learn how to manage stressful situations, we are learning how to exercise control over certain anxieties in a healthy way. We can remain focused and train our brains to problem-solve.

When we are experiencing prolonged anxiety, eventually the dopamine, norepinephrine, and serotonin levels drop significantly, almost like a crash (Stixrud and Johnson, 2019). This makes it very difficult to do or want to do anything. According to Control Theory, here is where we hit a wall after experiencing prolonged anxiety, and we feel we can't keep fighting this overwhelming feeling. We start not to care about things. We feel a loss of motivation. This is where depression starts to come into play. We are physically, mentally, and emotionally drained. We just can't keep fighting the anxiety anymore. This happens when we have been experiencing chronic anxiety. As Dr. Stixrud points out, this is the point where our dopamine levels drop significantly, and our motivation takes a major hit.

As described in Dr. Bessel van der Kolk's book, *The Body Keeps the Score*, our body experiences and retains information of life events, particularly traumatic events. Post Traumatic Stress Disorder (PTSD) is a sensory disorder, not a mental disorder. We become traumatized when we don't process the trauma we've experienced. The traumatic event itself is not what traumatizes us—it's not processing the trauma. Our body holds on to the trauma until it is processed. We need to be able to feel safe in our bodies before we can cognitively process the trauma endured.

To summarize, under chronic anxiety and trauma, the amygdala becomes overly sensitive and reactive. The insula becomes dysregulated (over or under active) and is quick to misinterpret information, providing incorrect information to the amygdala. The hippocampus starts to weaken, atrophy, and shrink. The cingulate becomes dysregulated making it difficult to focus and work with the PFC, and the PFC becomes weaker and under active, making us more vulnerable to becoming reactive and not able to reason logically and make sound decisions or problem-solve (van der Kolk, 2015; Stixrud & Johnson, 2018; Sweeton, 2019). Furthermore, when our kids experience anxiety for extended periods of time, the prefrontal cortex is not able to develop the way it should. This is extremely concerning, considering adolescents are too often experiencing higher levels of anxiety than adults and have a lower tolerance for stress than adults.

The objective here is to help ourselves and our kids understand our own anxiety and how to control it. We are teaching our kids tools that not only help them understand how to manage past stressors as well as manage stress in the moment, but also increase their confidence so that they will be able to manage stressors they come across in the future. Dr. Stixrud provides an exceptional description of how these theories apply to kids in our current time: "Chronically stressed kids routinely have their brains flooded with hormones that dull higher brain functions and stunt their emotional responses. Parts of the brain that are responsible for memory, reasoning, attention, judgment, and emotional control are dampened and eventually damaged… By teaching our kids these skills and increasing our sense of awareness, we are in essence immunizing our kids. We are preparing them to know how to manage anxiety in the future, therefore increasing their chances of succeeding in different areas of our life".

Understanding Triggers: Neural Networks

To understand neural networks, I'm going to start with describing more of the make-up of the brain and nervous system. Our brain is composed of billions of neurons, with each neuron connecting to and communicating with numerous other neurons, forming neural networks of information. Each network holds a vast number of memories, both implicit (subconscious) and explicit (conscious). Each network is built by life experiences, consisting of memories, sensations, people, environments, specific events, noises, smells, et cetera. (Sweeton, 2019). I like to think of neural networks like a map, with all the streets connecting the neurons, providing different information. To activate a neural network, there only needs to be one point of entry to activate the entire network (Sweeton, 2019). We don't need to activate each memory or sensation that comprises the neural network to activate the network. So, if I return to the same or similar environment where I previously experienced a high anxiety or traumatic event, that entire network will be activated, or triggered. Remember, we don't get to choose what our triggers are. Our brain, or neural networks, encode information from our experiences and how we interpret those experiences, and any part of those experiences that are part of an anxious or traumatic neural network could be triggering for us. Once again, our brain is wired in a way to keep us safe and alive, and when we become triggered, our brain quickly activates our stress response system in an effort to keep us safe. However, since we are vulnerable to misinterpreting what is happening, and if our amygdala is overly sensitive because we are consistently in a high state of anxiety, our hippocampus may struggle to provide context or accurate information to communicate to the amygdala that we are okay and safe in the moment.

Another concept that is important to understand is neuroplasticity, which is the mechanism of the brain and nervous system to reorganize neural pathways, connections, and functions (Sweeton, 2019). Dr. Sweeton presents six rules of neuroplasticity, which help explain what happens in our neural networks:

1). Neurons that fire together, wire together. Repeated experiences strengthen that network.

2). Use it or lose it. When neurons stop firing together, the neural network becomes smaller and weaker. Let's use the example of the map again. If you think about a town where you have lived for a significant amount of time, you likely know a lot about that town as far as street names, locations of stores or restaurants, how long it takes to get from your house to another place in town, back roads, main highways, et cetera. Think of that map as a strong neural network. The longer you live there, the stronger that map becomes, and continues to get bigger and stronger the more you learn about that town. However, if you move to a new town or city, you aren't going to know much (if anything) about how to get from one place to another, where specific stores are located, where the good restaurants are, how long it takes you to get to work at first, street names, back roads, et cetera. The map of your new town, or new neural network, is small and not very strong because you are new to it and haven't experienced much yet in your new town. However, this map/neural network will get stronger and bigger each day you spend there, traveling through town and building upon your experiences. Not only is your new neural network of your new town getting bigger, but your map /network of your old town starts to get weaker and smaller because you are not using that map/network on a daily basis. Over time, you might start to forget some of the names of streets in your old town, or the names of some of the restaurants or stores you used to go to, or what street to turn down to get from one place to the next, because you aren't using or activating that network on a regular basis anymore. You are activating your new neural network on a daily basis now, which will continue to get bigger and stronger due to your daily life experiences.

3). It's a two-way street. Brain change can be positive or negative changes.

4). Your attention is the network that you are in. Whatever you are thinking about or focusing on is the network that you are in.

5). State to Trait: Repetition and practice/effort promotes brain change. By practicing specific techniques (which I will present further in the reading) for 15 minutes/day for 15 weeks, brain structure will change.

6). Brain change is active, not passive. There may be things that help us calm or relax our bodies, but without us putting conscious efforts into our work, we can't expect our brain to change.

With trauma, the networks are very rigid and resistant to change. The networks are also fragmented (as discussed when talking about memory and what happens to the hippocampus under severe anxiety and trauma). Trauma networks are easily activated/triggered, and it is hard for someone to get out of that negative headspace/network (Sweeton, 2019). The trauma network is also isolated from other networks. It doesn't fit in or make sense with other networks, making it more difficult to find a way out of the network. The goal (in therapy) is to build a bridge from the negative trauma network into healthier, more adaptive networks. Trauma networks are impervious to new information or influence from more adaptive networks. The practice of Eye Movement Desensitization and Reprocessing (EMDR) facilitates the process of building a bridge to form or attach to another adaptive network from the trauma network. But to desensitize the trauma network, it first must be activated. As the rules of neuroplasticity state that your attention is the network you're in, and brain change is active, not passive, the traumatic network needs to be activated for it to change. However, with trauma, before doing any cognitive restructuring to start building new, healthy, and adaptive neural networks, we need to focus on working with the body to calm the nervous system first. EMDR incorporates working with and feeling into the body while activating the trauma network, as well as feeling into the body when forming healthier networks. I will discuss more about working with and feeling into the body in further detail as we go along.

Now let's tie what we know about neural networks back into our cognitive work. The goal of our cognitive work is to build and strengthen positive neural networks, while weakening and desensitizing our negative neural networks. We want to connect the negative networks with positive networks. This is where our cognitive restructuring takes place. Through cognitive restructuring, we start to identify when we might be misinterpreting information and start to understand our experiences from other perspectives, helping us build new positive and adaptive neural networks. Trauma networks are extremely immersing and all encompassing. Understanding or seeing other perspectives is impossible, and our thoughts are irrational when we are trapped in one, negative or traumatic network (van der Kolk, 2015; Sweeton, 2019).

Based on what we are experiencing and the context surrounding the experience (a social situation, taking a test, being in an unfamiliar place, being around people you don't trust, et cetera), our interpretation of that experience will prompt our body to react, either engaging the SNS, SRS, or impulsively reacting behaviorally. However, if the experience or stressor isn't extremely intense or strong, and the SRS is not yet activated and our frontal lobe is still online, we are still vulnerable to misinterpreting the situation. Our interpretations often lead to what I refer to as automatic thoughts. Automatic thoughts are defined by Judith Beck as "the actual words or images that go through a person's mind, are situation specific, and may be considered the most superficial level of cognition" (Beck, 2005, p. 16). According to Judith Beck, these automatic thoughts are based on our core beliefs, which we cultivate throughout our development and life experiences, particularly in the earlier stages. But first, let's start at the neuronal, subconscious level.

Core Beliefs and Attachment

Judith Beck's theory of core beliefs laid the foundation for understanding much of our automatic thoughts. According to Judith Beck, these core beliefs are global (not situation specific), rigid (very difficult to change), and overgeneralized. These are beliefs that we internalize when we are young, based on our experiences and relationships and how we perceive and interpret our environment, represent how we then perceive ourselves as individuals. These interpretations reflect the neural networks in our brain, which include information about our sensations, memories, past experiences, et cetera. Depending on whether a child has a positive or negative experience at a certain time or event of their life, that experience will influence how that child interprets their own sense of self, based on how successful they felt they were in managing that event or future events.

Core beliefs can also develop based on how we interpret information or feedback from others. These experiences form core beliefs that we can potentially maintain throughout much of our lives and may not be correct, which influences our own self-esteem or sense of self-worth. When we have negative experiences, it is easy for us to interpret these experiences in a way that has a negative impact on our sense of self. We often *assume* we are at fault. We start to have negative thoughts about ourselves, feeling as though we are not good enough or are a failure. We believe these thoughts are true, and we internalize them as part of who we believe we are as a person, forming a negative sense of self, and forming and building upon a negative neural network of who we believe we are.

Aaron Beck (1964) distinguishes between two different types of core beliefs: beliefs about ourselves and beliefs about others. I have found in my own practice that both types of core beliefs are equally common. A core belief that we might have about others can also stem from our early childhood experiences. We might believe that "no one is trustworthy" or that "other people will hurt me." Aaron Beck refers to these core beliefs about others as "generalizations." We need to understand the context of these beliefs and identify if these thoughts are valid or not based on supporting evidence. These core beliefs are likely to have repeatedly influenced our perceptions throughout our lives, so we can identify a pattern of when these core beliefs trigger our automatic thoughts, triggering our anxiety.

Attachment is also critical in the ways in which we form neural networks when we are younger, that directly influence how we interpret our environment and how we form (or avoid forming) relationships with others throughout our lives. A healthy attachment cycle looks like the following:

Child's needs → Express emotion or behavior → Need met → Established
(crying, reaching, talking) by caregiver **TRUST**

By experiencing a healthy attachment cycle, a child learns that relationships are predictable, they experience lower arousal (amygdala becomes stabilized and less sensitive or reactive), they are able to learn and engage in affect regulation and experience that relationships are safe and trustworthy (van der Kolk, 2022; Pressley, J., 2022). When babies are born, they have a larger amygdala because the brain is wired and primed for survival. As the baby's needs are met by their caretaker and they are starting to learn that their needs are being met and they can feel safe, their amygdala shrinks and is less sensitive because they know they will get their needs met.

On the other hand, when a child's needs are not met, they learn that relationships are not safe and aren't predictable:

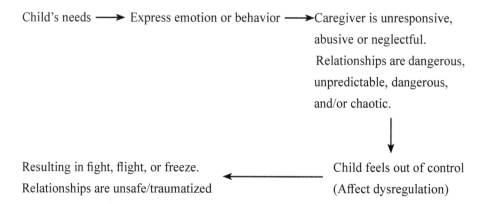

Child's needs ⟶ Express emotion or behavior ⟶ Caregiver is unresponsive, abusive or neglectful. Relationships are dangerous, unpredictable, dangerous, and/or chaotic.

Resulting in fight, flight, or freeze. ← Child feels out of control
Relationships are unsafe/traumatized (Affect dysregulation)

As a result of an unhealthy or traumatized attachment pattern, the child does not learn how to feel safe in their environment. Their brain remains extremely sensitive to their environment, remaining in a state of survival readiness. Their amygdala does not decrease in size as it would with a health attachment but remains in a state of alertness to keep the child safe. They are likely to develop unhealthy attachment styles as they develop, which may include those of an avoidant attachment style, anxious-ambivalent attachment, or a disorganized attachment.

An avoidant attachment style is developed when caregiving is chronically rejecting or withdrawn. The child learns to "over-control" their emotions where they minimize or cut off emotions, or "deactivate" attachment needs (Ainsworth, 1978). A child might believe, "I can't get my real needs met, so I better not show them," or "I better not expect too much from others." An anxious-ambivalent attachment style develops when the caregiver is inconsistent, is mis attuned to emotions and face to face interactions, is sometimes distant, neglectful, or intrusive (Ainsworth, 1978). The child cycles between seeking contact and angrily pushing away the caregiver. The child cycles rapidly between positive and negative emotions, and may believe, "I better exaggerate my needs to make sure someone will be there for me." Last, a disorganized attachment is developed when caregiving is either frightening (abusive), or frightened (lack of protection, neglected, traumatized caregiver). The caregiver is both the source of safety and danger (Main & Solomon, 1986). This attachment style is most connected with severe, traumatized development and chronic fear. The child often adapts by "controlling" other people or situations, and often looks like oppositional defiance, attention deficit, aggressive behaviors, or a more severe diagnosis.

Children often sacrifice or lose their sense of self for the sake of being loved and approved by someone in position of authority (Blowby, 1982). Again, they are giving others control over them. Children are primed to connect with their caregivers through eye contact, facial expression, tone of voice, physical contact, and are therefore able to establish a form of communication with their caregivers. Based on these attachment styles, you can see how feeling a lack of control prompts anxiety from the very start. The brain is wired to protect us and will react according to the environment and relationships in our lives. The healthier, more predictable the attachment, we develop a healthy personal sense of control with our caregivers and in our environment. The stronger the attachment, due to the caregiver's responsiveness, the more likely the child will be able to develop healthy relationships with others. However, our brain quickly learns when we are not getting our basic needs met and will adapt to protect us the best way it can, and looks for ways in which we can have some sense of control in our chaotic environment.

Let's apply attachment to core beliefs. If a child is abused at an early age, they are not likely to understand why the abuse is happening but can very easily start assuming that they deserve to be hurt because they did something wrong, they are not worthy of love and affection, they aren't good enough in some capacity, et cetera. These are core beliefs that quickly develop based on a child's early experience. As the child gets older, they might assume that others perceive them the same way, so any experience that reminds them of having been abused will trigger the same thoughts, which triggers their anxiety. They will often assume that they are not good enough, or they might think they deserve to be mistreated by others. Our negative core beliefs also directly affect our self-esteem and sense of self.

Additionally, someone who has a history of being abused might assume throughout their life that others (especially others who hold a similar relationship or dynamic as the child had with their abuser) will also abuse them. They might be constantly anticipating how others will react to them or treat them. They generalize their core belief that they can't trust people if they get too close to them or if they allow themselves to be vulnerable with another person.

Another example of developing core beliefs is when a young child experiences a loss in the sense of abandonment. If a child is placed in the care of others who were not their initial caretaker, especially after having already established a firm attachment with their initial caregiver, the child may then anticipate being abandoned by other caretakers or by others with whom they try to establish a relationship throughout their development and adulthood. Children who are adopted or spend time in foster care often struggle to allow themselves to fully engage in a relationship with a caretaker or other relationship, in fear of losing that significant person. It is common for a child who has not had the same caretakers their whole life, even as they continue to get older, to *assume* that they will be abandoned by others. They are likely to have a difficult time allowing themselves to fully engage in a relationship (romantic, friendship, or otherwise) without anticipating that the other person will leave them.

Even deeply ingrained core beliefs, however, are not necessarily true. Aaron Beck thought it was important to educate people about this—even when someone feels very strongly about something, it might be a false belief. Their experience is always valid, but they may be helped by learning to look at the concrete evidence for or against their automatic thoughts. We need to practice looking at the concrete evidence that may or may not support the automatic thoughts in a more logical way, without discounting how a person felt or feels. When we are able to identify examples of when someone experienced an event when there was evidence to prove that their core beliefs or automatic thoughts were not true, we can then work to modify core beliefs and automatic thoughts. We also heal negative attachment cycles through forming adaptive, functional relationships, forming an alliance. Much of this work is initially done by working through the body (which will be discussed later) and helping us feel safe in our own bodies before doing any cognitive work, and being able to neurologically connect with others. Our goal is to switch neural networks, from staying in a traumatized network of attachment to forming new, healthy relationships.

Automatic Thoughts

Our negative core beliefs develop as we internalize negative thoughts or assumptions. They make us vulnerable to experiencing anxiety and a limited sense of control. We quickly and easily go back into those old, negative neural networks. We are more apt to *assume* negative things in vulnerable situations. To identify automatic thoughts, it is important to take inventory of what is happening in the moment we start to feel any anxiety. Judith Beck stresses that when our mood changes, we should ask ourselves what we are thinking about in that moment. Remember the rules of neuroplasticity, that in order to make changes in our brain, we need to activate the old, maladaptive networks in order to start forming alternative, more adaptive networks. If we are not able to identify the automatic thoughts that are triggering our anxiety outright, we should do an inventory of the situation: "Where am I? What is happening? Who am I with?" We should continue to question our automatic thoughts by asking, "What am I anticipating? What am I afraid of happening? What is my biggest concern or fear?" We also want to check in with or pay attention to how our body is physically feeling. Are you noticing any tension or pain anywhere when the negative network is activated?

These assumptions or anticipatory thoughts will trigger our anxiety. We assume we are helpless; therefore, our sense of control is minimized. When we assume something negative, we believe the assumption to be true, and one automatic thought/assumption will trigger another and another and another. Soon, we are thinking about the worst-case scenario. We become consumed by these thoughts, prompting our helplessness or fears of impending disaster, and believe that these automatic thoughts are true or that they are *definitely* going to happen.

That's what anxiety does. It completely consumes our thoughts and focus. We become hyper-focused on these thoughts, which prevent us from being able to focus on what is actually happening in the moment. It prevents our cingulate from being able to focus on what we need to do in the moment and communicate with our PFC on coming up with a plan for what we need to do. The insula becomes dysregulated and is vulnerable to misinterpreting information or our environment. However, those thoughts are often not accurate or valid. We don't always have evidence or proof to show that those thoughts are absolutely 100 percent true or that negative situations are *definitely* going to happen. When we become consumed with these thoughts, they take control of our minds. We are so intensely focused on these thoughts that we struggle to focus on what we need to be doing in the moment or identify what is actually within our control. These automatic thoughts make it more difficult to focus on problem-solving or to identify what our priority is in that moment. That's how easily anxiety is triggered and how quickly it can intensify.

We want to pay attention to what we are thinking about in the moments leading up to our anxiety. We want to identify our automatic thoughts that are triggering the anxiety. This takes practice. Because we are not always consciously aware of what we are thinking, we have to try to identify or pay attention to any possible worry or concern that is causing us stress. What are we anticipating? What are we afraid of happening? Identify all those "what if?" statements. The more we pay attention to our thoughts, the easier it becomes to identify our anxiety-provoking automatic thoughts.

Once we are able to identify these triggering thoughts, we want to ask ourselves, "Do I have any evidence to prove that these thoughts are absolutely true or that something bad is definitely going to happen?" If we don't have proof that our automatic thoughts are absolutely true, we want to then shift our focus to what we are doing in the moment. We need to focus on what our priorities are and manage one thing at a time: "What am I in control of right now? What's the first thing I need to do right now?" This is the cognitive work. Here is where we are exercising our cingulate and insula, to become better regulated and stronger, allowing us to interpret more accurately what is happening and better able to problem-solve. We are training our brains to think differently than the way they've been used to thinking throughout our lives. We are reconditioning our brains to think in a more logical, step-by-step manner, and our brains aren't used to doing this on their own. Our brains naturally feed into those anxiety-provoking thoughts that then take over our focus. We are now trying to shift our focus from those anxiety-provoking thoughts to what is actually happening in the moment.

Other examples of assumptions or anticipatory thoughts that we often take on (or internalize, developing core beliefs) and therefore trigger our anxiety include, but are not limited to:

→ Fear of being judged, scrutinized, embarrassed, rejected, offending others, et cetera.

♦ Fear is a sensory response to a real or perceived threat (van der Kolk, 2015). If we are fearful of something happening, we are not going to feel we have control in that situation.

→ Anticipation of a future threat

♦ Again, if we feel threatened in any way or anticipate something threatening, we will not feel we have control or will feel that the control we have might be taken away.

→ Misinterpreting information

♦ Leading to assuming something that may not necessarily be true.

→ When things do not go as planned

♦ If something does not turn out the way we expected, our sense of control drops. We need to be able to accept that plan A did not work out and identify other options that we can use instead or identify another time when we will be able to pursue plan A. If we are able to accept that things did not go as planned and shift our focus to what our other options might be, we are increasing our sense of control in those given circumstances, rather than perseverating on what went wrong and continuing to feel angry or upset by the current circumstances.

→ Any changes occur, particularly unexpected changes

→ New experiences

→ Environmental factors (e.g., noises, crowds, activity)

→ Not taking accountability for our actions/decisions

♦ If we justify our behaviors/choices, blame others, manipulate, or make excuses as to why we acted inappropriately or made a mistake, we are not taking the correct steps to control the situation.

→ Not accepting what is not within our control

♦ Counterintuitively, accepting or embracing the fact that some things are out of our control can actually be empowering and freeing, a weight lifted off our shoulders.

Each of these precipitants will be addressed in greater detail later in the book.

Let's look at some other examples of how core beliefs are developed and lay the foundation for our automatic thoughts. Here is an example of a young child, Jane, who accidentally spills her milk at the dinner table. The spill itself can surprise anyone at the table, which can spark a host of reactionary responses. The mother, who happens to be sitting at the table, reacts in a negative way, such as shouting the child's name or exclaiming, "Jane! Come on! Why did you do that?" Jane might interpret that situation in a way where she assumes she did something bad or wrong and may assume that she disappointed her mother. Jane might also think that what she did was stupid or clumsy; therefore, *she* is stupid and clumsy. Even though her mom did not state in those words that she is stupid or clumsy, Jane may interpret her mother's reaction as such and is vulnerable to believing this about herself. Jane is likely going to place more value on her mother's immediate reaction rather than recognizing that it was an accident, that she didn't intentionally do anything wrong, and that her mother was just frustrated at the situation and reacted poorly. Children, like adults, are more likely to remember how someone or an event made them feel than what was specifically said to them at the time.

They are also likely to assume that if someone reacts to them in a shocking or aggressive manner, that they must have done something to deserve it. Because they don't have the life skills and experience to know otherwise, they assume that what another person is telling them is true. Young Jane might never express her thoughts—younger kids tend not to speak up about how they are feeling or how they interpret a situation as they may not yet have the tools to do so—but she will likely internalize certain assumptions based on her experience. If she has enough similar experiences, these assumptions could form a core belief about herself, which she will carry for the rest of her life, further strengthening that negative neural network of experiences and beliefs.

As a result, Jane, as well as any other child, is very vulnerable to internalizing negative thoughts about themselves. If Jane never speaks up about how she is feeling or what she is thinking, these negative thoughts will not be corrected and will form her core beliefs of who she feels she is and how she identifies herself. Children will start to form a negative sense of self rather than a positive sense of self, which would allow them to feel they were able to exercise a greater sense of control (even though kids are not consciously aware of this development). As children continue to harbor these negative core beliefs throughout their development and into adulthood, any vulnerable situation that taps into their core beliefs will automatically trigger (false) assumptions that they are a disappointment, stupid, not good enough, a failure, et cetera. These beliefs can stay with them and affect how they see themselves and how they approach challenges throughout their lives.

If I've always believed that I've been a disappointment to others throughout my development, then I'm going to continue to generalize this belief and assume this is true in other aspects of my adult life. I'm going to assume that I'm a disappointment as a spouse, as a parent, as an employee, as a friend, as a daughter, et cetera, even if evidence suggests otherwise. These negative core beliefs and assumptions will impede my ability to focus on what I am capable of accomplishing, to believe that I'm good enough as I am regardless of accomplishments, or that I actually have the ability to exercise control in my own life.

Another example of how core beliefs form the basis of our anxiety is if a child, Rebecca, gets a grade on a test or in a class that was less than what her parents desired. Rebecca's parents might respond in a way that highlights a lack of accomplishment rather than focusing on what she was actually able to accomplish. "Why didn't you get an A? Didn't you study enough? "What grades did your classmates get?" These questions are examples of the detrimental comments we often make to our kids regarding their academic performance. Rebecca can interpret these comments and questions as "I'm not smart enough. I didn't work hard enough. I'm not as smart as my classmates," as well as "My parents are disappointed in me. I'm not good enough for them. They think I'm stupid. I'm not doing enough"

If our kids interpret these experiences in such a negative way, specifically reflecting on how they are stupid or not good enough, or if they feel they failed their parents, they are then vulnerable to internalizing these thoughts, forming core beliefs, and believing these thoughts are true about who they are as a person. They can easily carry these core beliefs with them throughout their lives until they are able to identify them as flawed beliefs or have other corrective experiences that prove these beliefs are not, in fact, true, allowing them to develop a new, adaptive neural network. Let's fast-forward to when Rebecca is an adult. If she grew up internalizing the message that her performance in school was not good enough or that she hasn't accomplished what she should or what's been expected of her, she may become highly focused on accomplishments. She might try to prove her worth by being the best student, super mom, super employee, et cetera and not realize that she is good enough and doesn't have to kill herself trying to be perfect, an unattainable goal. If Rebecca is not exceptional at everything she does, she might easily interpret what she does or who she is as a failure.

Even though our anxiety is often rooted in core beliefs that were developed when we were young, anxiety can also be triggered by circumstances that may not necessarily be related to our core beliefs or sense of self. An example of how easily anxiety can be triggered and quickly escalate is a student who has a test tomorrow. Jack doesn't feel prepared for his math test. The first automatic thought that pops into his head is "I'm going to fail the test." That automatic thought can trigger the next thought and so on:

"If I fail this test, I'm going to fail the class.

"If I fail this class, I'm going to fail this semester.

"If I fail this semester, my GPA is going to drop, and I'm going to have to take summer classes. I'm not going to graduate on time. Colleges aren't going to want to accept me. I'm a failure as a student, which means I'm going to fail in other areas of my life."

See how easily those thoughts can snowball and escalate the anxiety? Our mind quickly takes us to the worst-case scenario. Jack's anxiety in this example may not necessarily be rooted in his core belief system but was triggered by the circumstances surrounding the issue; Jack was not prepared. However, if Jack developed negative core beliefs when he was younger based on having experienced negative or critical feedback from his parents or teachers, like the example presented earlier with Rebecca, then Jack's negative core beliefs could trigger anxiety that is not just based on circumstances but is more deeply rooted. Jack might assume he will fail his exam because he is not smart or because he feels he is a failure. He may be more focused on these core beliefs than on recognizing that the anxiety might just be due to the circumstance of not being prepared, therefore limiting his ability to focus on what is actually within his control or to recognize that these beliefs might not actually be valid. Jack doesn't have proof that he will *definitely* fail the exam, but he struggles to recognize this or understand how his anxiety is affecting his functioning.

Some automatic thoughts have an obvious source, like not feeling prepared for a test, but others are harder to explain. For example, you might be sitting on the couch after a long, tiring day at school or work. You finally get a chance to relax, but you suddenly start feeling intense anxiety. You may even have a panic attack, but you have no idea why. It feels as though it came out of nowhere. You are not able to identify any automatic thoughts in the moment because the anxiety is too intense.

Although it might feel as if the anxiety comes out of nowhere, you are feeling this way for a reason. You want to find the source of this anxiety. After the anxiety starts to subside, think back to what you were doing five or ten minutes prior to when the anxiety started. How were you feeling then? Try identifying what you were thinking about at that time. What were you doing? What were you anticipating? Did something you saw, heard, smelled remind you of a time when you experienced high anxiety? We want to tap back into that old, negative neural network in order to work through it.

If you have trouble identifying the triggering automatic thoughts, keep backing yourself up, hour by hour, trying to identify what you were doing and what you were thinking about at the time the anxiety started to set in or what you were doing prior to when you started to feel anxious. Try to recall about what you were thinking. Keep working your way back along the day's timeline until you are able to identify a stressor that potentially triggered the anxiety. Once you work your way back far enough to where you recognize that you were feeling OK and the anxiety wasn't affecting you, think about what might have happened or changed between the time you were feeling OK and when you started to feel anxious. You really want to focus on the automatic thoughts, which can easily be triggered by random experiences throughout your day, including things you see, hear, smell, or taste, location, environment, people, or responsibilities.

So why do our anxiety or panic symptoms set in out of the blue? Sometimes we might actually have experienced something that could trigger our anxiety earlier in the day, but the anxiety doesn't become overwhelmingly intense right in that moment because we are focusing on our other responsibilities throughout the day. Because we experience so many things throughout our day, much of what we experience is not fully processed by our brain in the moment but is put in the back of our mental filing cabinet. Instead, our brain prioritizes what we are in the middle of doing or what we are anticipating having to do in the immediate future. We don't spend a lot of time processing every single experience or stimulus with which we come in contact throughout the day.

When we sit down at the end of the day to relax and the anxiety sets in, oftentimes our brain is playing catch-up and processing more information about what we experienced throughout the day. Our brain is now reviewing what we previously put in our mental file cabinet. Our anxiety might not have been triggered in the moment we saw someone who looked like someone from our past who would typically spike our anxiety; we were likely more focused on what else had to be done, so we didn't think about it too much. But once we sit down to relax at the end of the day, we start to feel panic. It feels like it came out of nowhere. Our brain is still processing what we saw and experienced earlier in the day, so our anxiety doesn't intensify until our brain is able to process more information.

I had a client we will refer to as Katie, who was a college student and worked a part-time job. She described having a panic attack at the end of the day, after getting home from school and work. Katie described her anxiety as though it were completely random. She wasn't doing anything unusual or thinking about anything that made her particularly anxious and struggled to understand why she would have "random" panic attacks at the end of the day. I had her think back, hour by hour, about what she was doing and how she was feeling. She described how her day went, including what was being discussed in each of her classes at school. Katie felt her classes went well, and there were good topics and conversations throughout her day.

I asked what topics had been discussed in class. In her criminal justice class, they had watched a video of a man in prison who was in solitary confinement because he was suicidal. When she shared this information with me, she stopped talking. She recognized that the word *suicide* was what triggered her earlier in the day, but the class discussion continued, and she didn't spend much time focusing on that word in the moment. She then went through the rest of her day, not having processed that her anxiety had been triggered, and because she hadn't focused much on that word or topic in the moment, her brain continued to process that experience well after the fact, which eventually triggered a panic attack.

Once Katie was able to identify the source of her anxiety and the reason for her panic attack, she actually felt a sense of relief. She was able to gain some understanding of her anxiety instead of continuing to feel as if it had come out of nowhere or there was no reason for it.

Fear of Rejection and Loss

Another significant factor that tends to precipitate avoidant behaviors is the fear of rejection. As we discussed regarding attachment, rejection can have a significant impact on how we view the world and interpret our place in it with others. Most people do not want to feel rejected in any aspect of their lives. It's a painful and embarrassing feeling. Where is our sense of control when we experience rejection? It's very low. We feel we have a limited sense of control in circumstances where we feel vulnerable and rejected. Think about what is happening when we are rejected—another person is making a decision that affects us. We are not making that decision ourselves. Someone else is making a decision for us. It's not within our control yet we have to accept the decision that is being made. If we were the ones making the decision, we would have control and therefore would not feel rejected. No one wants to be rejected. We all want to be the ones shaping our own destiny and who makes the decisions, but that's not reality in every situation.

Examples of when we might anticipate rejection include someone for whom we have feelings; family members leaving; moving between foster homes; and being rejected by a school we wanted to attend, a job for which we interviewed, or a social group. We don't like when situations do not go the way we would like, especially when we feel our "selves" were being deemed not worthy of love, inclusion, acceptance, et cetera. Separation anxiety and fear of abandonment are examples of when a child anticipates losing or being separated from a significant attachment figure in their life. When a child is fearful of losing an important person in their life, the child does not feel confident that that person will always be in their life, and their sense of personal control over that relationship is minimized. Unfortunately, rejection can have a lasting effect on us. Our assumptions can easily take complete control over our minds, and we quickly start thinking of the worst-case scenario when anticipating being in a vulnerable position. Rejection can also be difficult to accept when that early experience of rejection was so significant that it resulted in our internalizing negative core beliefs about ourselves.

Young children are constantly trying to live up to the expectations of their parents, caregivers, teachers, et cetera. They are very focused on what others think and feel about them. They want to please others and do what makes others happy and to feel that others "approve" of them. Unfortunately, this can come at a cost. It's good that kids try to do well by others, don't get me wrong, but they often become so focused on what others think of them that it becomes all consuming, and this mind-set can impede a child's ability to focus on their self.

An example is if a child, Susie, feels she doesn't get as much attention as her brother, she might feel rejected. Susie might assume that there is something wrong with her or that she is unlikable or unlovable, that she doesn't deserve attention or any kind of special treatment. Kids want to please their parents/caregivers and will often do whatever they can to make them proud. They might feel that if they are able to please their caregiver, maybe their caregiver won't reject them, at least not in that moment. Kids will often try to please others in order to feel accepted. They become more concerned about upsetting others, not fitting in with others, and being rejected than they are about themselves and what they feel is in their own best interests. As previously discussed, these assumptions can easily be internalized, essentially becoming part of the child's core beliefs. The child could also generalize these beliefs to other aspects of their life throughout their development or assume that if they disappointed their parent once or twice, that they will always be disappointing their parent or others.

Another example is if Charlie doesn't get invited to Jake's birthday party, knowing that a lot of his friends were invited. He could very easily assume that Jake doesn't like him, that he did something to make Jake mad and not invite him, or that other kids don't want him there. He might also start to compare himself to his peers, thinking or assuming that he isn't as much fun as the other kids, he's not as likable, he's not as smart, et cetera. It is extremely hard for kids to focus on themselves or recognize what is actually true when faced with stressful social situations. Charlie struggles to recognize that, if he didn't do anything wrong, then it's on Jake (or Jake's parents) as to why he wasn't invited, and he shouldn't feel bad about himself.

Because kids don't always verbalize what they are thinking or feeling, these negative and personal assumptions can easily become rooted as core beliefs if they are not addressed. These core beliefs will then continue to trigger anxiety as we get older. If Charlie continues to believe that he is not well liked by others as he gets older, he will likely assume or anticipate not being invited to other parties or social gatherings, generalizing this assumption to be true of any future social engagement. He might avoid engaging with others if he anticipates being rejected in any way and continues to internalize that he is unlikable or that others don't want to be around him. These core beliefs will then easily trigger anxiety in other areas of his life, such as when he tries out for a sports team or a play or applies to college or for a job. He might assume that he is not going to make the team or land a role in the play, that he isn't going to get accepted into the schools of his choice, or that an employer won't want to hire him because he is not a likable person. Even if Charlie has worked hard throughout his schooling or career and has applied himself to the best of his potential, he will more likely focus on the negative core beliefs instead of recognizing his other strengths and qualities. He will have a difficult time not comparing himself to others and will assume that no matter the circumstance, he will continue to be unlikable, potentially limiting himself in taking risks, applying for jobs, or pursuing new relationships or friendships.

So how do we deal with rejection and manage potential rejection? Here is where we want to identify any automatic thoughts that are triggering our anxiety. We need to identify what we are afraid will happen, anything that we are anticipating or assuming to be true. We then want to review these thoughts to see if there is any evidence that these thoughts are *absolutely* true.

- Do I know for a fact that I'm *definitely* not going to get the job for which I applied?
- Do I know for a fact that I'm not a likable person and that others don't like spending time with me?

- Do I have *proof* that if I don't make the team, it's because the coach doesn't like me and doesn't want me on the team?
- Do I know for a *fact* that I'm not capable of becoming a decent ballplayer or that I won't be able to learn and succeed at a new job?
- Do I have *proof* that I have been a bad friend to make others not like me?

Where is the evidence? Kids can't do this themselves; they need a parent to reassure them of their inherent worthiness.

If we don't have proof to show that any of our automatic thoughts are true or that they are *definitely* going to happen, then we need to practice shifting our focus to what we know to be true and what is currently happening. We want to shift our focus to what we know we're capable of doing and what we've already been able to accomplish (providing evidence against our assumptions) and, most importantly, focus on ourselves. Again, here is where we are building new, adaptive networks. Each time a negative neural network is activated, we want to recognize that it's activated and identify the flawed thought, and bridge over to the new neural network by asking ourselves the questions presented, building a new adaptive network, and focusing on ourselves. We do not want to compare ourselves to others, because doing that can make us more vulnerable to thinking and internalizing negative thoughts about ourselves.

Once again, when we compare ourselves to others, we are giving others control over us. We are allowing others to influence how we feel, what we do, and how we act. We are not focused on ourselves and what we need to do that's in our own best interest. When we are able to focus on ourselves, we shift that control back into our own hands. We want to continue focusing on our own strengths and skills, reiterating what we are capable of accomplishing as well as the evidence that shows we have already been able to succeed in various areas of our lives. This is our new adaptive neural network.

It is important for us to work hard and identify personal goals for ourselves, reflecting growth in areas we value. For example, we still need to work hard in school or apply ourselves as best we can to do well at work. But we also need to stay focused on our own strengths and skills rather than comparing ourselves to others. When we start comparing ourselves to others, we become vulnerable to assuming negative thoughts about ourselves or feeling that we aren't as good or as smart enough as others around us. It is also our choice regarding which areas we want to master. We don't have to play baseball or join a band because we think it's "cool" or because that's what we think others want us to do. We can pursue what is meaningful to us. It's our choice, no one else's. Sometimes people find themselves trying to win a race they didn't even want to run.

For example, even if I don't get the job for which I applied, I know that I can still be successful at another job or in the same field. That job, or not getting hired for a job, does not define what I'm capable of attaining. If I don't do well on the SATs, that doesn't mean that I won't get accepted into a good school or be successful in my future. If I can stay focused on what I know I can do and continue to hold myself accountable for my own responsibilities, knowing that I'm doing my best, then I will be more capable of accepting that I didn't get into the school of my choice. I know that I'm a good student. I work hard, I'm dedicated, I take school and work seriously, all of which gives me more evidence that I can and will be successful in school and work because I know what I'm capable of accomplishing. I'm not going to let a test score, a school, or a job determine if I will be successful. They do not define me. Rejection does not define me. Granted, it is still important to take accountability for the things I need to work on, improve my skills, and accept and utilize constructive feedback. Simultaneously, I need to stay focused on the fact that I'm choosing to hold myself accountable for these areas of progress and know that I can still be successful in what I pursue. I'm the one defining who I am and what I can accomplish. I have the control.

Regarding relationships, if we're anticipating being rejected by someone for whom we have feelings, we should try to stay focused on what we ourselves are capable of providing in a relationship. If someone chooses to not be with us from the outset, and we did nothing to hurt this person (at least not intentionally), then we need to recognize that it is their choice to not engage in the relationship. However, their decision does not indicate that we are not engaging, that no one would want to be with us, or that we won't be able to establish and maintain healthy and successful relationships. It is their own personal choice, which is separate from who we are.

We also have to accept that we can't control another person and "convince" them to be with us. We need to stay focused on who we are, independent of the other person. Furthermore, if that other person chooses not to be with us, we need to be mindful that we don't give that person control over us to the point where we change who we are to meet their needs or please them in ways that are not true to ourselves. We want to know that we are presenting our real selves, and if other people choose not to engage with us, that's their choice. Again, we need to practice shifting the focus back to ourselves, review the strengths and qualities we have independently, and not let that rejection define us or take away from our own sense of control.

We can also experience rejection after having been in a relationship for a significant period of time. Let's face it—not all relationships are lasting, yet no one wants to feel rejected by their significant other. In this case, we still want to focus on ourselves and our role in the relationship. If we know that we did everything we could to try to make the relationship work, such as actively communicating and listening to and supporting the other person to the extent that we could, then we did the best we could. However, we have to recognize that we are not independently responsible for making the relationship work; the other person is equally responsible.

On the other hand, if we did something that hurt the other person in the relationship, we need to take accountability for our actions. Our partner may or may not forgive us, but if we take full ownership of our choices and understand what we need to work on moving forward, then we are following through with our responsibilities in the relationship. We can't undo what we did, but we can take accountability for the choices we made and the choices we make moving forward. If our partner then chooses to end the relationship, even after we have taken full ownership of our actions, then at least we know that we did what we could after the fact. This means we managed the situation as best we could, but we need to accept our partner's decision to end the relationship. Our focus should then be on the fact that we took accountability for our actions and did the best we could to mend the relationship, what we learned, and what we can do moving forward in our future relationships.

A study conducted at Duke University (Psychology Today, Oct. 2017, p.55) used a scale that measured the extent to which people would go in order to be accepted by others. Although it is beneficial to feel a sense of belonging in some capacity, that longing to belong to a group can also come at a cost. Dr. Mark Leary of Duke University stated of their research that, "People who are higher in the need to belong may have greater problems saying no because of concerns about rejection. They also might have a strong fear of negative evaluations, so they worry that saying no will cause others to judge them unfavorably. People are concerned about the disappointment, frustration, or inconvenience that their refusal might cause" (Flora 2017). I have found this to be very common in my own clinical work.

It can be costly to our sense of self when we are highly focused on what others want, how to please others, how to meet others' expectations, or how not to upset anyone. If we say no to someone when taking into account what we need to do for ourselves or what is in our best interests, and the other person becomes angry or upset, we can validate their feelings and let them know that our intention is not to upset them but that we have to do what's right for ourselves, even if the other person does not agree. It is the other person's job to accept that they don't have control over others and that situations are not always going to turn out the way they want. Others are not always going to do what we want or agree with us all the time, and we have to learn to accept that fact. We are not responsible for managing their feelings, just as they are not responsible for managing ours.

Even in instances when we are willing to help others and do what is asked of us (specifically when it is not interfering with our taking care of our own responsibilities), it does not mean that the other person decides how and when we do things. We are still able to have a say in how we help others. For example: "I would be happy to help you move into your new apartment, but I won't be able to stay all day. I can come in the morning or even help you pack, but I have to be back home by a certain time to take care of other responsibilities." We can create boundaries, so others don't walk all over us. I will address boundaries to a greater extent in the discussion of communication.

One last example comes to mind regarding rejection. I came across a story on National Public Radio's *All Things Considered* (2017) about a gentleman named Christian Picciolini, who is the founder of a group called Life After Hate. Christian is a former white nationalist who spoke out about the violence in Charlottesville, Virginia, in August 2017. He provides an example of how people, particularly young people, have a need to belong and to feel accepted. Being accepted into a group is often a way to prevent feeling rejected and, in this case, a vehicle to become violent. Christian has been working to reform white nationalists through his organization. He made a very valid point, saying, "I think ultimately people become extremists not necessarily because of the ideology. I think that the ideology is simply a vehicle to be violent. I believe that people become radicalized, or extremist, because they are searching for three very fundamental human needs: identity, community, and a sense of purpose." He goes on to talk about experiencing abandonment when he was younger, which led him to this community. (This is also remarkably similar to how others can become involved in gangs.) He states that a lot of younger people often feel lost and don't have much hope and end up searching for "very simple black-and-white answers."

This example speaks directly to the point of Control Theory, in that it is extremely easy for us to allow others to exercise control over us (whether it's intentional or not) when we don't have a strong sense of self or self-esteem. If our self-esteem is low and we don't have a strong sense of who we are individually, our anxiety is automatically high. It's extremely easy for us, especially as children or adolescents, to follow what others do or to make decisions that we feel will win the approval or acceptance of others. Once again, we give our control to others rather than being responsible for ourselves. We aren't focused on who we are as individuals or what is important to us personally. Our focus is on what we think others want of us, and we make decisions that please others rather than those that are in our own best interests. It is very easy to lose our sense of self and self-control when our driving forces are a fear of rejection and the need to belong. This provides another example of why it is so critical for us as adults and parents to teach our kids healthy ways to exercise control and strengthen their personal sense of worth through learning responsibility and accountability.

What Do We Do When We Recognize That Our Automatic Thoughts Are Not Valid?

Once we identify the automatic thoughts that prompt our anxiety, we need to evaluate the validity of these thoughts. Following Judith Beck's recommendations, we would question what evidence we have to support these thoughts. After we identify the automatic thoughts that are triggering our anxiety, we need to ask ourselves, "Do I have any evidence or proof that these thoughts are real? That they are *definitely* going to happen? Where is the evidence?" When we don't have any proof that these assumptions or anticipatory thoughts are absolutely going to happen, the thoughts are not necessarily valid.

Once we recognize that our thoughts may not be valid, we then want to shift our focus to what we are doing in the moment. Rather than continuing to allow these automatic thoughts to have complete control over our focus, reactions, behaviors, et cetera, we want to shift our focus from those automatic thoughts to what we are doing in the moment. We need to ask ourselves, "What is my priority *right now*? What are my responsibilities *right now*? What is in *my* best interest *right now*?" We need to focus on ourselves and what is actually happening in the moment. Our focus needs to be on what is within our control in that moment, not on all the "what ifs?" that we have no proof will definitely happen.

As we work on shifting our focus from the automatic thoughts to what we are doing in the moment, we are training our brain to think differently than what it's used to. This is the work of the cognitive therapy. We are reconditioning our brain to think in a more logical, step-by-step way, which our brain doesn't typically do on its own. Our brain naturally feeds into the anxiety and allows the anxiety to take complete control of our focus. We become so consumed by our anxiety-provoking thoughts and negative beliefs that we struggle to focus on what we need to do in the moment, our behaviors/actions, and what is actually within our control. Again, our aim is to strengthen the cingulate and insula. The cingulate helps us re-focus and come back to the present moment, helping us to problem-solve.

Shifting our focus from our automatic thoughts to what we are doing in the moment and what we are in control of in the moment takes practice. This is work that we need to do consistently throughout the day to become the masters of our thought processes and not to let them operate on autopilot. We are training our brains to get control of the anxiety-provoking thoughts. We are no longer allowing our anxiety to control our thoughts or what we do. We are taking control of the anxiety by becoming more aware of it, understanding more about what triggers it and where it's rooted, reviewing if our thoughts are valid or not, and shifting our focus to what is within our control.

Judith Beck lists additional questions to evaluate automatic thoughts; however, this is where Control Theory diverges from Cognitive Theory. I recommend shifting our focus to what we are doing in the moment after identifying whether or not these automatic thoughts are valid. I feel it is important to shift our focus to what we *can* control, given the circumstances. Again, our goal is to recognize what is within our *control*.

Let's go back to Jack, who was worried about taking a test the next day. If Jack is able to identify and review his automatic thoughts about taking the test and recognizes that he does not have any evidence to prove that his thoughts are valid, that there is no proof to say he is *definitely* going to fail the exam, we want him to shift his focus back to how he is doing in the present moment. In that moment, he's not failing the exam. In that moment, he's OK. None of his automatic thoughts are happening. He's OK in the moment. Our job is to shift our focus to what our priority is in that moment after identifying our automatic thoughts. However, a more valid thought for the student might be "I'm afraid I won't do well on my exam because I'm not prepared." This actually leads us to our next step.

What Do We Do When Our Automatic Thoughts *Might* Be Valid?

If we review our automatic thoughts and find that we are antic-ipating that something will happen because it's happened before, then those automatic thoughts have some validity. Again, we don't have proof that those anticipatory thoughts are *definitely* going to happen, but if they do, we want to be able to focus on what we can do to manage the potential situation as best we can. We want to identify options that are within our control to manage the potential situation. In other words, we want to problem-solve.

Jack, from the previous example, might assume he will fail the test tomorrow because he previously failed a test in that class or with that teacher. In that case, there is some validity to his concern. He might also be anticipating failing the exam because he does not feel prepared. This is also a valid concern. If our automatic thoughts are valid or could potentially happen, then we want to come up with a plan or identify op-tions that are within our control to help manage that potentially stress-ful situation to the best of our ability. If Jack is worried about failing the test, let's identify some options that are within his control to help prepare as best he can. Keep in mind that even though we are creating a plan to manage the potential situations as best we can, we still don't have proof that he will definitely fail the exam. Some options that are within his control might include:

- Carving out time in his schedule that night so he can study
- Reviewing his notes or previous tests from that class

- Reviewing a study guide
- Reviewing the chapters on which he is being tested
- Calling a friend to review some questions
- Making flashcards
- Reviewing vocabulary
- Doing some practice problems

When we are anticipating something that could potentially happen, we want to focus more on problem-solving than continuing to perseverate on our automatic thoughts, which may not ever happen. (And are more likely to happen if we are paralyzed with fear!)

To do this, we want to start by coming up with plan A that we can implement if a potentially stressful situation presents itself. If plan A doesn't work, go to plan B. If plan B doesn't work, have a plan C.

START: Identify Plan A

```
Does Plan A work?  ──────▶  Yes  ──────▶  Great!
        │
       No  ──────▶  Identify Plan B
                            │
                    Does Plan B work?  ──────▶  Yes  ──────▶  Great!
                            │
                           No  ──────▶  Identify Plan C
                                                │
                                        Does Plan C work?  ──────▶  Yes
                                                │
                                               No
                                                │
                            Keep identifying options that you can work
                            with.
                            Keep your focus on what is within your control.
```

The objective here is to identify options that are within our control and focus on problem-solving. By training ourselves to focus on what is within our control and to identify what our options are to best manage the stressful situation in the moment, we are increasing our sense of control over the situation. As we continue to focus on what our options are, we are training ourselves to engage in more forward thinking and to recognize what is within our control, rather than staying stuck and focusing on what is wrong or not going the way we want. This is important for kids to learn to do, as they are prone to thinking in black and white, all or nothing terms, and need to learn how to problem-solve. They need to be taught how to look for other options that may be in the "gray area." Kids quickly assume the worst-case scenario but often don't know how to get out of that anxiety. If we teach them how to problem-solve, we are helping them train their brains to focus on what is within their control, stopping the SRS, stopping the release of cortisol, and activating the PNS to calm the body back down, recovering from the anxiety.

Also, when we focus on what we can do moving forward, we won't be caught off guard as much as we would be if we didn't come up with a plan. We will have already thought through what we can do and will feel more prepared. If we feel more prepared, we will feel a greater sense of control. If we feel a greater sense of control, our anxiety will automatically start to come down on the scale as our confidence and sense of readiness and security increase.

This is also where we exercise *flexibility in thinking*. We are trying to train ourselves to shift our focus away from what we cannot control toward what we can do in the moment. Control Theory aims to focus more on what we can do in the situation, using practical skills and giving ourselves a greater sense of control.

Just because something does not work out the way we want or intend does not mean that we are failures or can't be successful. We must learn how to accept what doesn't go our way while still holding ourselves accountable for focusing on what else we can do moving forward. One way to help accept what we don't have control over is to ask ourselves, "What is my responsibility right now?" If we can't change the circumstances we are facing, we want to then shift our focus to what we can do in the moment. What is plan B?

Let's revisit the example where Jack is assuming he is going to fail his exam. In addition to focusing on what his options are to help prepare as best he can, given the time constraint, he might also try accepting that potentially getting a C on the exam is an acceptable goal because getting an A may be unlikely if he didn't have a lot of time to prepare. We want to practice being flexible in our expectations, given circumstances that are not within our control.

Anticipating the Next Panic Attack or Anxiety Episode

It is very common for people who have had severe anxiety or panic attacks to constantly be anticipating when the next one will happen. This anticipation is another example of how easily we can get caught up in our thoughts and assumptions about something that might not ever come to fruition. However, because of our history with anxiety and panic attacks, the anticipation of another attack has some validity. When we assume that we are going to have another anxiety or panic attack, that thought takes control, and it is exceedingly difficult for us to focus on what we are doing in the moment. We struggle to recognize in the moment that we are OK. We need to train ourselves to focus on the fact that we aren't currently having a panic attack and are safe, healthy, et cetera.

Unfortunately, we continuously anticipate: "What if this happens? What if that happens?" Those thoughts trigger more automatic thoughts about what else might happen if we have a panic attack, and soon we are focusing on the worst-case scenario. Those thoughts have taken control of us once again, and we struggle to focus on how we are doing or what we need to do in that moment, to be mindful or present.

When we focus so much of our attention on the "What ifs?" we struggle to focus on what we are actually doing in the moment. We might be doing something absolutely benign, but we allow ourselves to get caught up in the automatic thoughts that trigger anxiety. Our brain quickly misinterprets that experience as us being unsafe or that something is not OK. Here is where we want to recognize that we are having automatic thoughts if the anxiety isn't high enough to trigger the stress response system. We need to identify those thoughts and review them to see if they are valid. We need to ask ourselves if we have any evidence to prove that these thoughts are *absolutely* true or that these fears are *definitely* going to happen. Do we know for a fact that we are *definitely* going to have another panic attack in the near future? If there is no evidence to support the automatic thoughts, we want to shift our focus from those thoughts to what we are doing in the present moment. We want to focus on what is within our control and what our priority is in that moment, rather than focusing on the "What ifs?" that may not ever happen. We want to recognize that we are safe in that moment.

However, when we are anticipating an anxiety or panic attack, we often *assume* that because we previously had a panic attack, we're going to have one again. When we base our assumptions on past experiences, it's hard to convince ourselves that it's not going to happen again. Our past experience provides evidence that the experience could, in fact, happen again. In this case, we want to identify what we can do if that situation recurs (if we do have another panic attack) to help us best manage that potential event. Now, we still don't have proof that we are *definitely* going to have another panic attack in the near future. However, by identifying options that we can utilize should an attack arise, we are increasing our sense of control over the situation. We are getting the automatic thoughts back under control and bringing our anxiety down by creating a plan of action.

For example, if I'm anticipating having a panic attack when I'm in a public setting, I want to identify options to help manage it. Where can I go if I start to feel anxious? Can I step outside and get some space away from the crowded room? Is there someone I feel comfortable talking to if I need to? Maybe I can leave an event early if I become too overwhelmed. I can even lock myself in a bathroom if I need a couple of minutes away from others. These are all options that are within my control.

Keep in mind that we don't want to avoid engaging in social or other events that might trigger anxiety (assuming we aren't engaging in anything too dangerous). Even if we leave an event early, at least we were able to make it to the event. Once there, we should continue to gauge how we're doing from time to time, focusing on how we're able to maintain control in the present moment. (I will address avoidance in detail when discussing defense mechanisms.) Once we can identify options or come up with a plan to help manage that potential situation, we then put that plan aside and shift our focus back to what we are doing in the moment. We need to keep training ourselves to stay focused on how we are feeling in the moment, what we are doing in the moment, what is currently within our control, and what our primary responsibility is at that time. We need to recognize that, in that moment, we aren't having a panic attack, and we are still in control and are safe.

It can be difficult, particularly at the start of our work, to shift our focus from the automatic thoughts to what we are doing in the moment or what our priority is right then. Again, our brains naturally feed into our anxiety-provoking thoughts because it is a natural defense mechanism, better suited to escaping predators than dealing with work deadlines. It's the fight-or-flight reactive response when we feel threatened or feel we do not have sufficient control.

Unfortunately, we can quickly and easily become completely consumed by these automatic thoughts, to the point where it is very difficult to stop focusing on them. In order for us to shift our focus from the automatic thoughts that consume us to what we are doing in the moment, we need to continuously practice this skill until it becomes natural. The cognitive exercises that we will be building on train our brains to think in a more logical, step-by-step manner. The cognitive approach conditions our brains to think differently than they are used to with regard to anxiety. Our brains naturally react to their environment in a defensive manner and feed into our anxiety. This cognitive approach gets easier the more you become familiar with and practice it, but it can take some time to adjust your approach.

Sense of Self and Self-Esteem

Self-esteem is one aspect that is directly affected by anxiety. To better understand this, let's go back to the scale. When our anxiety is high on the scale, our SRS is activated, the SNS is activated, and our sense of control is low. Self-esteem goes hand in hand with our sense of control. Think about your own confidence when your anxiety is high. If you don't feel you have the level of control you need in a particular situation, your confidence and self-esteem are likely to also be low.

When our anxiety is high, we are vulnerable to negative beliefs, such as *"I'm not good enough. I'm not smart enough or as good as others. I'm a disappointment. I'm a failure."* Once again, we are stuck in the negative neural network, and the more time we spend here, the stronger and bigger that network becomes. We are vulnerable to internalizing these thoughts if we don't feel we have the level of control that we need or want. If we feel we know what we're doing and have evidence to prove that we're capable of doing or accomplishing something, then our sense of control is going to be higher with regard to that aspect of our lives. Our anxiety will therefore be lower, and our self-esteem and confidence will be higher with our increased sense of control as we develop and continue to strengthen a new, healthy, adaptive neural network. We are not going to be as vulnerable to having these negative thoughts and beliefs if we know what we are capable of and have a higher level of control in a certain area of our lives. Self-esteem isn't just about feeling good about ourselves; it encompasses understanding ourselves to a greater degree and knowing who we are and what is personally important to us versus who we think others want us to be.

Our sense of self and self-esteem can be analyzed by identifying recurrent themes within our automatic thoughts and neural networks. These themes will likely stem from the core beliefs that often build the foundation for our anxiety-provoking thoughts. Aaron Beck talks about the ways in which we distort information, creating what we have been referring to as automatic thoughts. The way in which we interpret information can be influenced by our core beliefs. Aaron Beck refers to these themes as "cognitive distortions." He lists several of these—all-or-nothing thinking, catastrophizing, emotional reasoning, et cetera—

which Judith Beck also includes in her work. Although these thought distortions can differ, there is a common theme among them, which is a lack of sense of control. There is a theme of lacking self-confidence or a positive sense of self within these cognitive distortions; they are based on assumptions or anticipatory thoughts, and they lend a feeling of helplessness or hopelessness, which, again, is lacking a sense of control. Cognitive distortions can also develop due to the hippocampus (memory center) becoming damaged by prolonged anxiety or trauma. If the hippocampus is providing fragmented information, we are vulnerable to misinterpret what is happening because we don't have an accurate context from which to draw that would allow us to make accurate conclusions.

After identifying and evaluating automatic thoughts, Judith Beck focuses on formulating new beliefs. According to Judith Beck, many of our core beliefs are not necessarily truths but are ideas that can be changed or modified. I find this theory helpful and relevant to our own work with automatic thoughts, specifically for those who often present with rigid, all-or-nothing thinking. Some of these beliefs or ideas that Judith Beck presents in her work have been very common in my work with clients:

"If I don't do as well as others, I'm a failure."

"If I ask for help, it's a sign of weakness."

"If I fail at work or school, I'm a failure as a person."

"I should be able to excel at everything I try."

"If I don't live up to my potential, I have failed."

"If I don't work hard all of the time, I'll fail."

"If I show my emotions or cry, I'm weak."

At the root of these thoughts are core beliefs, which also lay the groundwork for our self-worth. If we had negative experiences as a child which we interpreted as letting down someone important in our lives (such as feeling like we disappointed our parents), we may have misinterpreted that experience; therefore, we become vulnerable to believing that we are not good enough or that we didn't live up to our parents' expectations in a more universal sense. If we don't talk to our parents about these thoughts and feelings (as children very rarely do) and don't receive any feedback to help correct our interpretation of that experience, help us understand that we did not fail but that maybe we made the wrong choice, and help us learn from the situation, we will likely carry this core belief with us into other areas of our lives and throughout our development.

If we grow up believing that we're never going to meet anyone's expectations or that we're going to fail at most things we pursue, we will continue to experience high levels of anxiety and automatically take on negative assumptions in different areas of our lives. We will have a difficult time feeling confident that we will be able to succeed, or at least not fail or suffer a humiliating outcome, in whatever we try. We will also have a harder time accepting that, even if we don't perform up to the level we were expecting, it does not mean that we're failures or that we won't be able to accomplish our goals.

Furthermore, we need to think about what our goals and values are. Our primary goal should always be to do our best. If we know that we are doing our best, then we are doing our job. Simultaneously, we want to be flexible with ourselves if we don't perform better than others around us. We are not failures if others have outperformed us when we know we did the best we could. We can still hold ourselves accountable and continue working hard to improve our skills. We need to become aware of our automatic thoughts, as well as to explore the underlying core beliefs that lay the foundation for these thoughts. When we increase our level of awareness of our thought processes and beliefs, we are better equipped to evaluate the validity of these thoughts and prevent ourselves from internalizing negative, self-deprecating thoughts.

Let's review where our anxiety is when we are flooded with automatic thoughts. When our minds become consumed by automatic thoughts, our anxiety quickly becomes higher on the scale. When our anxiety is high on the scale, our sense of control has dropped. Again, if we felt we had more control over a given situation, we wouldn't be as vulnerable to assuming or anticipating something that may not ever come to fruition, and therefore our anxiety would not be as high on the scale.

So where is our self-esteem when all this is going on? When we don't have a healthy, strong sense of control over a situation or over one or more aspects of our lives, our self-esteem also drops. When our anxiety is high on the scale and our sense of control is low, our self-esteem is right down there with our sense of control. They go hand in hand. As we start to exercise more control over a situation or one or more aspects of our lives, our self-esteem is going to increase. As we see more evidence that we are effectively communicating or setting boundaries with others, and as others are starting to respond to us more appropriately, we're going to feel our sense of control increase, as well as our confidence, as we're seeing for ourselves that we're doing the work and creating the positive changes we desire. We're going to feel more confident in ourselves that when another stressful situation arises, we will know what we're capable of doing or what we need to do. We will feel more prepared and more confident and have an increased sense of control.

An example of how our self-esteem suffers as a result of our anxiety is when we are dealing with social interactions. It is very common for people to experience heightened anxiety in social situations. When we are interacting with others—more specifically, people with whom we are not necessarily well acquainted—we tend to presume how others are perceiving us. We often start focusing automatically on what others think of us, leading to automatic thoughts such as, *"Do they like me? Am I making a good impression? Do they think I'm smart? Do they think I'm interesting? Do they like how I look? They think I'm stupid. I'm so annoying. They don't want to talk to me. They're not going to want to hang out with me again."* The thoughts go on and on.

If we're already assuming that these thoughts are true, our sense of control is quickly lowered, if it wasn't already low before, and our self-esteem is also low. We aren't going to feel confident in ourselves or be fully engaged in the social situation if we are so focused on these negative automatic thoughts, potentially leading to the negative impression we were worried about making.

Body image is another area that is affected by the way in which we perceive or interpret information and feedback from others, affecting our self-esteem. A lot of people, especially adolescents, are highly focused on what others think of them and try to look a certain way in order to be accepted, approved, or not judged negatively. We also see so much in the media and society in general that emphasizes the need or expectation for everyone to look thin and stylish. When it's constantly in our faces, it's hard to ignore.

Unfortunately, our anxiety can easily feed into the need to meet others' expectations, including those of people we don't even know. Again, this is why it is so critical for us to focus on ourselves and what is in our own best interest. When we place so much focus on others' expectations and allow others to influence what we do, what we wear, what we eat, or how much we weigh in ways that are not healthy or appropriate, we are allowing others to have a level of control over us that is not serving our best interests. In those moments, when we make a choice to dress a certain way or control what we eat so that we can "fit in" with others or be "accepted," we are exercising a false sense of control. Our anxiety might decrease slightly on the scale, but it's only temporary, and we're not exercising healthy control of ourselves. We need to focus on what is right for ourselves, what makes us feel comfortable and authentic, not what we think others expect of us or what society tells us we should look like.

We are in control of our own bodies, no one else. It is not up to anyone else what we do, what we eat, what we wear, how much we weigh, or how we present our sexuality or gender identity. We need to focus on how we exercise control over our own bodies and on taking care of ourselves. If we don't fit a certain societal mold, but we know that we're taking care of ourselves in the way we need to and staying focused on making most decisions in our best interests, then we are doing our job. It's not up to anyone else to control our choices or how we take care of ourselves. If we are too focused on how others are judging us with regard to our physical appearance, our sense of control drops, and our self-esteem also takes a hit. If we're allowing others to influence how we look in order to feel approved or accepted—in other words, to control us—then we're not exactly feeling confident in ourselves, thus limiting our self-esteem.

Additionally, if others care so much and feel the need to judge us, it speaks more to their own anxieties, insecurities, and limited self-esteem and is not our anxiety to hold. Here is where we need to be mindful of when it may not necessarily be our anxiety but someone else's. In that case, we are not responsible for managing others' anxieties. We are responsible for taking care of ourselves, and our own health, not someone else's anxiety. This is important to recognize; that we often take on the anxiety of others, assuming it is our own anxiety or insecurities, and make decisions based on how we think others would accept or approve of us. We aren't focusing on ourselves and what is in our own best interest.

For those who have battled disordered eating and are in recovery, think about how your way of thinking has changed since you last engaged in disordered eating. What are you focused on with regard to your own body and health? It's common for those who are in recovery to learn to appreciate their bodies as they are: that they don't have to look a certain way or a way in which society tells you. Think about what is happening in this change of thought. You are shifting your focus from them to you. You are taking back your personal sense of control that was once lost to others by trying to look the way you thought others wanted you to or weigh what you thought was acceptable to others.

When we are so focused on what we think others want us to look like, wear, or weigh, we are essentially giving them our personal sense of control. When we shift our focus back to ourselves, we are taking back that control. We are deciding that *we* have control over our bodies, not anyone else. We are not allowing others to control what we look like. We learn to love ourselves for who we are and recognize that we are not going to let others make decisions for us regarding how we look or feel about ourselves. We stop allowing others to have that control over us, and we learn to exercise healthy control for ourselves. We learn to stay focused on ourselves and appreciate ourselves. When we are too focused on what others think of us, we often lose sight of what makes us unique. We let others destroy what makes us special. However, when we shift our focus back to ourselves, we stop allowing others to take away or minimize what makes us unique. We learn to appreciate who we are individually, and we will not let others define who we are or who we should be. (Eating disorders are also a type of defense mechanism and are common when there is a history of trauma, which I will address further in the reading.)

Lastly, if others can't accept that we look different from them (including in ways that are not within our control, such as skin color or other physical attributes), then they are responsible for accepting that they can't control others and that not everyone is going to agree with them or be who they want us to be. Here is another example of where we need to set a mental boundary for ourselves, recognizing that others have to learn to accept what is not within their control and to focus on themselves as well. It is not our job to look or present ourselves in a certain way to fit another's expectations. Even if others are not able to accept what is not within their control or focus on themselves, it's still important that we at least set a mental boundary for ourselves, knowing that we are not doing anything wrong if we don't meet someone else's expectations. Again, if we are taking care of ourselves in the ways that are in *our* best interests, then we are doing our job. We are the only ones who control how we take care of our bodies and how we present ourselves, no one else.

Meeting Expectations

Expectations, those of others as well as our own, can be very stressful and anxiety provoking. Young kids frequently try to please their parents, caregivers, teachers, and other important adult figures in their lives. Expectations can also stem from our core beliefs. By becoming more aware of our core beliefs, we are better equipped to catch our automatic thoughts and less likely to misinterpret feedback based on our core beliefs (not assume the worst or that someone is only giving us negative feedback). Our focus on body image might not even start in adolescence. If we are exposed to information relating to body image or hear comments about how we look when we are young, we can easily misinterpret that information and start to internalize negative (automatic) thoughts about ourselves.

If a child hears someone who is important to them making comments about how they or someone else looks, or even makes a comment to the child about their appearance, the child can easily interpret these comments in a way that is damaging to their own sense of self. They start to form a negative neural network about themselves from a young age. The child may start to wonder if that person they idolize disapproves of how they look. These early experiences, depending on how a child interprets them, can start to mold their core beliefs that others won't approve of them. These core beliefs will continue throughout their development until the child, adolescent, or even adult becomes aware of how their beliefs have affected their sense of self and recognizes how these core beliefs have been triggering negative automatic thoughts in any circumstance where they feel vulnerable about their appearance. Until we gain awareness of these core beliefs and their impact on our anxiety, our sense of control remains limited.

When we focus on ourselves, we are working on building our sense of self-worth. We learn about our own strengths and weaknesses and what we are capable of accomplishing. When we are more focused on ourselves, we are better equipped not to let others' judgments interfere with or exercise control over what we need to do for ourselves. We also learn not to compare ourselves to others. Comparing ourselves to others shifts our sense of control from ourselves to them, making us vulnerable to putting unrealistic expectations on ourselves. When we do not meet these expectations, we often interpret this as a failure. Focusing on our needs is not the same as being self-centered. It can help us appreciate that the way in which others act, dress, et cetera is their way of meeting their own needs. We can then accept each other as unique individuals.

Another example of how we often allow others to have control over us is when we anticipate how others might react to something we say or do. Oftentimes, we will avoid doing or saying something because we are afraid of upsetting another person. Our intention is not to upset anyone, but it is important that we can express what we need to say. However, when we avoid doing or saying something because we are anticipating how another person will react, we are giving them our control. This includes people-pleasing and not saying "no" so that others don't get upset.

Referring back to the scale, our anxiety increases when we anticipate how that person is going to react, so if we avoid that conversation or behavior, our anxiety will temporarily go down on the scale, once again giving us a false sense of control. Unfortunately, our actual level of control stays low because we are still allowing that other person to hold the control and influence what we do. Eventually, that anxiety is going to go back up on the scale because we didn't actually manage the situation and exercise control in an effective manner. We weren't focusing on ourselves but on others' potential reactions (although we have no definitive evidence of how they will react) and therefore letting go of our own sense of control. (I will address avoidance at greater length when discussing defense mechanisms.)

One critical example of how expectations can spike anxiety is when adolescents are undergoing the college application process. Ask any student nowadays what their experience has been when thinking about what colleges to which they will or have applied. This process has changed significantly since the 1990s and early 2000s. Students are under extreme stress when going through this process: starting with just thinking about what schools they will apply to, their SAT/ACT scores, their GPA, what level classes they take, how many extracurricular activities they are involved in, being captain or top athlete on their sports team, getting scouted by different schools, applying for scholarships, and the list goes on. (Not to mention the pressure that parents often place on their kids to get into a top school.)

This is just the tip of the iceberg when students are preparing for college. The underlying automatic thoughts on which the students perseverate are guiding them to make decisions that may not necessarily be in their best interests or even make them happy. Students are taking on expectations from others all around them. They are more focused on what others want them to do than on what they feel is right for them. They want to make their parents proud and get accepted into top-tier schools. *They constantly compare themselves to their peers*, which leads them to feel or assume that they are not as smart as their peers based on their grades or test scores. They assume they won't get into as "good" a school as their friends, which further leads them to assume that they won't be as successful as their peers, they won't get a good job, be able to buy a home, et cetera and that others will perceive them as failures. When students are constantly comparing themselves to their peers or focusing on what they think their parents, teachers, or others want them to do, they are essentially giving others control over their decision-making processes and their lives. They are only focusing on what they think others want or expect them to do, rather than focusing on themselves and what is actually in their best interests.

It's also common for students to view this process in all-or-nothing terms: "If I don't get into the school of my choice, then what's the point of pursuing any school. I'm just a failure." Students have a very difficult time recognizing that if they don't get into the school of their choice, they can still choose another school and be just as successful and happy, perhaps even more so. But because a student doesn't get into their first-choice school, they automatically assume that they won't be as successful in life and that others will be better off.

We need to communicate with our kids and students that they are the ones in control of where they apply and what they pursue. They are becoming adults and need to exercise their own independent choices. Parents need to let their kids exercise this control. If students choose not to hold themselves accountable for their responsibilities (for example, they don't get their applications in on time), then they need to learn from the natural consequences. Parents cannot do the work for their kids, and by "work," I mean organizing their college information, filling out college applications, signing them up for SATs/ACTs, getting transcripts or letters of recommendations for their kids, doing homework for them, et cetera. Students need to focus on what is important to them personally and not what is important to others—peers or adults. If they are hardworking students and are able to hold themselves accountable for their responsibilities, then they are doing their job. Those skills and the ability to focus on themselves will transfer to other aspects of their lives, whether they attend college, go into the workforce, raise a family, et cetera. If students don't get accepted into the schools of their choice, it does not mean that they will not be successful in life. It does not mean that they will never get accepted into college. It does not mean they are failures. There is no evidence to prove that these will be the outcomes. They will be OK if they don't get accepted into their first-choice school. They are also capable of coming up with alternate plans if plan A or plan B doesn't work out.

Furthermore, students often allow colleges to exercise control over what they should be doing. For example, students take on the expectations of schools where they have to get a certain score on their SAT/ACT to be considered or they need to have a GPA of 3.8 or higher, and even students who have a 4.0 GPA are getting rejected from schools. This is absurd! A GPA does *not* define how successful a student is or will be later in life. However, students take these expectations to heart and feel that, if they don't have the GPA or test score a school is expecting, they are not good enough or, once again, a failure. Students are allowing colleges to have control over what they do with their lives, rather than focusing on what is in their best interests.

Students need to focus on themselves and ask themselves, "What is going to make *me* happy? Where do *I* want to go? What am *I* interested in pursuing in school or as a career? What am *I* passionate about? What do *I* want to explore?" It's not up to the college to determine if you are "good enough." I always encourage my clients to focus on how they can exercise control when interviewing with colleges or even jobs. Students need to ask schools (or at least think about), "What do you have to offer me? Convince me that I want to come to your school. What am I going to walk away with after my time at your school? How is this school/job going to help enhance my career and what I want to pursue?" Students need to shift the power of control from the schools to themselves. *They* are in control of their future, not the schools or anyone else. Regardless of what others want or expect from our students, they need to learn how to navigate the world based on their own choices and to focus on what is important to them, not on what they think others want from them.

Social Media

Another prime example of how easy it is for us to lose focus on ourselves, triggering severe anxiety and affecting our self-esteem, is social media. We are exposed to what others are doing, good and bad, and we make judgments about others, or we assume others are judging us. We are able to present to others what we want them to see and, therefore, allow others to control what we do or how we present ourselves. People frequently present their "best" moments on social media, and we then assume all their moments are amazing. We judge our "blah" moments against their top 1 percent moments. We are more focused on what others think of us than on ourselves. As we become more consumed with what others think of us, we are less able to develop our own personal sense of who we are. We base our sense of self on how we think others judge us or on assumptions we have of how others perceive us. Once again, we are letting others control who we think we should be and are not focused on ourselves or what is important to us.

A study found that when children, teens, and young adults consistently spend excessive time on social media, they feel increasingly lonely, tired, and left out (Twenge, 2017). A study conducted by Dr. Jean Twenge, author of *iGen*, focused on the impact of smartphones on adolescents between 2011 and 2012, when the number of those owning smartphones increased to more than 50 percent. She had started doing research on generational differences twenty-five years before. The study found the following:

- There was a significant increase in the number of kids who said they felt sad, hopeless, useless, that they couldn't do anything right, et cetera.

- An increased number of kids felt left out and lonely.

- There was a 50 percent increase in the number of cases of clinically diagnosed depression between 2011 and 2015.

- There was a significant increase in the suicide rate compared to prior years.

- Nearly 40 percent of eighth, tenth, and twelfth graders got less than seven hours of sleep.

- There was a significant decrease in the number of eighth, tenth, and twelfth graders spending time with their friends in person.

These findings are not surprising when applying Control Theory in how we perceive information. We automatically start making assumptions that are not necessarily true. We are more intensely focused on what others are doing or how we think others perceive us than we are on ourselves. When we see what others are doing on social media, we assume we were intentionally left out or that our "friends" did not want to include us. Here is what adolescents refer to as FOMO, or "fear of missing out." We become consumed by what others think rather than focusing on ourselves and what makes us happy. We end up acting in ways that are not true to ourselves. Our actions are based on what we think others want us to do, or we act in ways to please others rather than focusing on what's in our own best interest. When we aren't focused on ourselves, we don't feel we have the level of control we need; therefore, our anxiety automatically increases.

Older generations didn't typically know (at least not immediately) if there was a get-together that they weren't invited to. They didn't see pictures of each time people went out or engaged in social activities. They didn't put as much focus on what they looked like when they were hanging out with their friends because they were the only ones there, and they didn't have cameras in their pockets.

Consider bullying. We used to not have to worry about being bullied once we left school. Home was a safe place where we weren't bullied by our peers. Even if we were bullied, not everyone saw it. It wasn't exposed to everyone to humiliate us in the public eye. Now, everyone can see who's being bullied, and they often just follow what's happening or join in the bullying. It's a completely different world compared to even twenty years ago.

Cyberbullying has also been a significant catalyst for controlling and manipulating others. There have been several incidents in which cyberbullying has been a contributing factor in people committing suicide. Oftentimes, cyberbullies are exposing others' private lives, stripping people of their own personal sense of control. They use this personal information to blackmail or manipulate people to get what they want or simply to make others feel so vulnerable that it becomes excruciatingly painful and overwhelming, and they don't know what to do, leading them to take their own lives so they don't have to live under the extreme control of someone else.

Where does our control go in these instances of social anxiety? We are not focusing on ourselves. We are focused on what other people think of us and are allowing others to hold that control over us. We need to recognize our automatic thoughts when we find ourselves in stressful social circumstances and review these thoughts: Do we have any evidence or proof that these assumptions are *absolutely* true? Do we know for a fact that others *definitely* feel one way or another about us? We can't predict what others are thinking, and, more often than not, we don't have evidence to prove that others are definitely judging us in a negative way. Unfortunately, we become so consumed by these thoughts that we start to believe they are true before exploring any evidence to support them. Again, when our sense of control is low, our self-esteem also suffers.

Now let's use an example of a social scenario where we feel a stronger sense of control. Let's say we are going to a party for a friend. (This can be relevant for any age.) We may have an idea about who might be there because we know who our friend enjoys seeing socially. Not to mention that we will know the person we will be celebrating. There might be a little anxiety because we might not know everyone there, but we have an idea of who might be there that we know. We might even reach out to some of these friends before the party to see if they are going, giving us a better sense of who will be there. When we have more information about the situation we will be going into, we will likely feel more in control than we would if we didn't know who was going to be there or whether we would know anyone.

Just having a little more information about what (or who) to expect will give us a stronger sense of control. We will automatically have more of a plan of what we can do and who we can talk to at the party. If we know who we will be able to talk to at the party, we will be less likely to focus on how others may be judging us or to assume others are thinking negatively about us, and our anxiety will likely not be extremely high on the scale. We will also be less likely to distort or misinterpret social interactions if we know more about the people with whom we will be engaging.

We will be less likely to allow the influence of others to affect our own sense of self or our behaviors. We will feel more confident saying no to doing something we don't want to do, such as drinking or using drugs. When we know what to expect, our anxiety will be lower; therefore, we will have a better sense of control and be likely to feel more confident in ourselves. This makes sense when you think about meeting new people. Initially, we might feel a bit anxious when speaking with someone for the first time, but once we get to know that person better, we feel more relaxed because we know more about them and how we can relate to or engage with them. We gain a better sense of control.

Flexibility in Thinking

Because we are so vulnerable to misinterpreting or distorting information, we want to pay attention to these thoughts when we set out to attain a goal but are not able to meet our own (and oftentimes others') expectations. Just like with automatic thoughts, we want to evaluate these cognitive distortions to see if there is any evidence that these beliefs are valid or not. Our "all-or-nothing" thinking, "black-and-white" thinking, catastrophizing, generalizing, et cetera may not necessarily be valid. Once we can identify these thoughts or beliefs, we then want to identify alternative outcomes or explanations that could potentially happen.

Here is another example of where we are practicing *flexibility in thinking*. Flexibility in thinking is being able to modify our plans or options as needed. We are training our brains to think in the gray area. By exercising more flexibility in our thinking, we can focus on the pertinent information at hand, rather than on the potential negative feedback, allowing us to stay focused on ourselves, what we have accomplished, and what we are able to do moving forward, focusing on what is within our control and being able to problem-solve.

Just because we don't get an A on a test does not automatically mean that we failed or that we're not smart. We may have made a mistake and didn't catch it. We may have read the question wrong. Maybe we thought we were more prepared than we actually were. Maybe we were exhausted when we took the test and couldn't focus. We also want to focus on what we know to be true; that we are capable, smart, and can be successful.

In any case, we want to focus on what we learned from the experience. If we didn't get as high a grade as we would have liked or were expecting, we want to not just understand the possible reasons we didn't perform well, but also to identify what we can do differently next time. We want to focus on what we can do moving forward, rather than perseverating on the thought or belief that we failed. We also want to recognize that it is OK not to always get As on our exams. We can still make that a goal, but we need to allow ourselves to be more reasonable and *flexible* with our expectations of ourselves. If we don't get an A on a test, it does not mean that we're not smart or that we're a failure. We can still pass the class. *The test or grade does not define who we are or what we are capable of accomplishing.* We want to focus on the fact that we did what we could or the best we could in the situation. Granted, there may be times when we didn't put all our effort into doing the best we could and maybe slacked off, in which case we need to take accountability for these choices. (I will address accountability in greater detail later in the reading.)

An example of utilizing flexibility in thinking and a solution-focused approach is going about a typical day of work. We leave the house at the usual time, but while we are en route, there is an unexpected traffic standstill on a main road of our commute. Initially, we may feel frustrated as our usual routine is not going as planned. Here is where we have to accept that we don't have control over the traffic or what is happening on the road and shift our focus to what our other options are. What are some of the concerns (automatic thoughts) that pop into our heads when we first approach the standstill? We might first be wondering what is causing the standstill (and hoping that no one is hurt if there is an accident), but we might also be assuming that we will be late for work, and this could possibly ruin our morning.

Now we don't have proof that we will *definitely* be late for work, so let's shift our focus and identify the options that are within our control, given the circumstances. We could come up with another plan to get to work. By coming up with an alternate plan, our sense of control will increase, and our anxiety will automatically start to decrease. When we are able to be flexible in our thinking, we aren't so rigid and stuck on the fact that there is a traffic jam, and we don't continue to sit in the traffic feeling angry. If we are familiar with the area, we might know some back roads we can take to work. We can also ask for directions or use GPS. We can also call our employer to inform them that we might be late due to a traffic incident, so we don't worry about what our supervisor is going to say if we are actually late. This also prevents our supervisor from making assumptions about why we are late or thinking that we are being irresponsible. These are all options that are within our control when things do not go according to our initial plan.

Another example of focusing on what is within our control and using flexibility in thinking is when we want to exercise, but we have no energy or motivation. We might feel that if we don't put in a full-hour workout, there is no point in exercising at all. It's all or nothing. Here, as well, we need to modify our expectations. Instead of focusing on the all-or-nothing thinking, let's come up with a more manageable plan. If we don't feel like going to the gym today, maybe we can just work out for ten or fifteen minutes, then assess how we feel. If we're still too tired and don't have energy, we still got in ten or fifteen minutes of a workout instead of not going at all. If we feel good after ten or fifteen minutes, then we can try to do ten or fifteen minutes more, then see how we feel again. Instead of giving up from the start and not even attempting to exercise, we might actually prove that we're able to accomplish a lot more than we thought we could, just by challenging ourselves with small, manageable steps.

We can also apply this approach to studying or working. When we are presented with a big task or project, it might feel overwhelming. We might automatically question if we are capable of successfully completing this work. Even though the project might seem challenging, we don't want to assume that we won't be able to complete the project or do a good job. We don't have any proof of not being able to do the work. We may be challenged by our core beliefs or previous experiences when we might not have performed up to our or someone else's expectations, and therefore interpret that experience as a failure or assume that others did not feel we were suitable or smart enough for the job. We need to pay attention to these thoughts and ask ourselves if we have any evidence or proof that we definitely won't succeed with this project. Even though we might not have proof that we won't be successful, we still might feel overwhelmed. So how do we manage to take on such a big task? Break it down:

- Use a planner to schedule time each day that we can dedicate to working on the project. Laying out a schedule can help prevent procrastination. Within this schedule, we might even break our work down into smaller tasks. We might start with doing research one week, then coming up with an outline of how to present this information, then write the paper or construct the project, then use the remaining blocks of time to review the work and make any needed changes.
- Even during times of studying or working, we might have a hard time focusing. In that case, we can start out by doing twenty to thirty minutes of work, then take a break. Then go back and do twenty to thirty more minutes of work and take another break. Our natural attention span is actually quite limited. We are better able to refocus after taking a break and then coming back to the task at hand than if we try to force ourselves to focus for long periods of time. The way our memory works is that we are likely to remember more

information at the start of a study/reading period and the end. If we break our study or reading periods into shorter segments, we are increasing the amount of information we are likely to retain.

However, if we sit down to study for an hour or two hours straight, we will most likely remember more information at the start of that hour and the end, but there is a lot more time in the middle where we are less likely to retain as much information. When we break these study periods into smaller segments, we will still remember more information at the start and the end of those segments, but we are limiting the amount of information in the middle of that study period that we won't remember.

By identifying a plan, organizing our tasks, and managing our time, we have more control over managing the project. These are important objectives in managing larger tasks that initially feel overwhelming. When we utilize our organizational and time-management skills, our sense of control increases, which automatically decreases our anxiety and overwhelming feelings. As our sense of control increases, our confidence also increases. Our self-esteem and confidence are directly related to our sense of control. When we see ourselves accomplishing these tasks that we planned out and organized, we have evidence in front of us that proves we are capable of successfully completing our work and are building upon and strengthening our healthy adaptive networks while the old, negative network becomes weaker and smaller.

It is also important for us to focus on areas of success, accomplishments, and progress. We want to shift our focus from the negative core beliefs (negative neural networks) to any area where there is concrete evidence of progress or success (positive neural networks). Unfortunately, it is very easy to let the anxiety take control and focus more on our negative aspects and qualities than to pay attention to anything positive we may have accomplished. It only takes one small factor to trigger the entire negative network. Here are some examples on how we can modify our thinking to focus more on areas of success or progress:

- I really didn't feel like going to the gym today, but I was able to go for an abbreviated workout.
- I didn't clean the windows in the house today, but I was able to clean all the bathrooms, do the laundry, vacuum, and clean the floors.

- I didn't get as much work done today as I wanted to, but I was at least able to organize myself, so I am prepared for tomorrow and the rest of this week.

If we have a better sense of control going into the next day or the upcoming week, we will feel more confident in our own ability to succeed in our work. Unfortunately, it is very easy to lose sight of all the things we have accomplished or areas of progress. We tend to focus on the *one* thing that we didn't do or "failed" to get done.

These examples show how easy it is for us to interpret information in a way that impedes our ability to focus on what we are able to accomplish, recognize what is within our control, or understand that we did the best we could. It also points out how damaging it can be to our sense of self and self-confidence when the focus of the situation is on what we did *not* do, rather than what we were able to accomplish. When we repeatedly hear comments that focus on how we are not meeting others' expectations, we are likely to develop a thought pattern that becomes focused on what other people expect of us, which:

1) prevents us from being able to focus on ourselves,
2) makes us constantly change or modify our behaviors and what we say based on what we think other people want us to do or what we think they want to hear, and
3) allows others to ultimately control what we do.

We are not focusing on what is in our control or what we feel we need to do that is in our own best interests.

An exercise that I often recommend to my clients is to do a nightly self-check-in before going to bed, identifying all the areas of progress, success, and accomplishments throughout the day. These areas of success can be something small, such as:

- finally having the time to run to the post office
- scheduling an oil change for your car
- finishing a book
- making it to the gym
- making dinner
- taking a shower (Parents especially know what I mean!)

It can also be something big, such as:

- completing a large part of a project you've been working on for school or work
- doing a presentation
- taking care of your kids all day
- managing a classroom of kids
- running a race
- getting a promotion

We need to practice focusing on what we can accomplish and validate our strengths and accomplishments and the work we did to get there. It is important that we do not minimize the work that we do and how we have succeeded.

Focusing on Ourselves

The examples we've been discussing highlight one of the most critical tools for managing anxiety and increasing our personal sense of control, which is to *focus on ourselves*. This objective takes practice. It is so easy for us to focus on what others expect of us, making other people happy, not upsetting anyone or disappointing others that we forget to focus on ourselves. Remember, it is important to recognize that when we focus so much on what others want and not what we want, we end up acting in ways or making decisions that aren't necessarily in our best interests. By doing so, we are giving others control over us. If we allow others to exercise this control over us (even though it's not necessarily intentional on their part), we won't feel comfortable or authentic because we aren't acting on our own behalf. Therefore, our anxiety increases.

In order to help us focus on ourselves, we want to take inventory of our priorities and responsibilities. We need to recognize and remind ourselves that we are doing the best we can, rather than focusing on what others expect from us. Of course, there are still expectations of parents, caregivers, and teachers, and we still respect their expectations and work hard to understand their importance. At the same time, we need to stay focused on the fact that, while we will try to work hard, we are doing the best that we can, which means we may not always meet our parents', caregivers', or teachers' expectations, and that's OK, as long as we aren't behaving inappropriately or in destructive ways. It does not mean that we are not working hard or that we won't accomplish our set goals or meet those expectations all together. It doesn't mean that we don't care about their expectations or don't respect those who only want (or think they know) what's best for us. It does not mean that we won't be successful or that we are not good enough. (Here is where those core beliefs can influence how we perceive and interpret our experiences.) We need to be vigilant about our automatic thoughts and aware of the core beliefs that trigger our anxiety. We need to continue to evaluate those thoughts and practice shifting our focus to what we are able to do in the moment. *This takes practice.* Our way of thinking does not change overnight. We are essentially training our brain to think differently under stress than the way it typically has. *Again, this takes practice.*

When we are more focused on what others expect or want from us, we become less and less focused on who we feel we are, what is important to us, and what our own priorities or responsibilities are. It is critical that we are able to focus on ourselves and what is important to us, as opposed to what is important to others, because we need to develop our own sense of self. When so much of our focus is on others, we are not focusing on our own development. We can often feel lost or numb or not know what is important to us, what our passions are, or even what we want to do in our future. We want to help our kids learn how to focus on themselves at early ages. Yes, as I said before, kids will always work hard to please the adult figures in their lives, but we also want them to learn to recognize when it's important to focus on themselves in various circumstances, including with their peers.

As we respect the expectations of our parents/caregivers, parents also need to check themselves and let their kids make age-appropriate choices to develop problem-solving and accountability skills. It is natural for us, starting as young children, to work hard to please these important figures in our lives and make them proud. We *want* to live up to their expectations and make them happy.

However, as we become adolescents and young adults, we start to individuate from our parents and caretakers. This is a time when we are supposed to become more independent and think for ourselves, making more independent decisions, navigating social relationships and dynamics, and learning how to uphold our personal responsibilities. This does not mean that we no longer value what others want from us, but our focus needs to shift from doing things for others to doing what is right for ourselves. These choices that we make, whether they are good or bad, help shape who we are and our sense of self. We learn from these experiences. If we grow up consistently making decisions that we think others want us to make, even though those decisions may not be what we ultimately want or even what is necessarily in our best interests, we are not going to develop as strong a sense of self. In an effort to help individuate from our parents or caregivers, we want to try to stay focused on not just holding ourselves accountable for our choices and responsibilities, but also working hard and doing the best we can in what we are working toward.

Anxiety and Its Relationship to Depression and Suicidal Thoughts

It is very common for those who suffer from anxiety to also suffer from symptoms of depression, which is the leading cause of disability in the United States in people ages fifteen through forty-four. (Anxiety and Depression Association of America, 2015; World Health Organization, 2017). Suicide is one of the leading causes of death in the United States, the second leading cause in people ages ten through thirty-four (National Institutes of Mental Health, 2019; CDC, 2017). According to the latest World Health Organization (WHO) estimate in 2017, more than 300 million people are experiencing symptoms of depression, which is an increase of more than 18 percent between 2005 and 2015. The WHO speculates that the lack of support services for people who suffer from mental health problems combined with a stigma of mental health have been significant factors to preventing people from getting the treatment they need. This is where Control Theory can help destigmatize mental health and provide easy access and education, particularly within schools, to help decrease these numbers.

Understanding suicidal thoughts is critical; however, I'm not going to talk about crisis intervention. I want to emphasize the importance of how easy it is for someone to develop suicidal thoughts by way of anxiety and the overwhelming feeling of not having a sense of control in one's life. Suicidal thoughts should *always* be taken seriously. We want to be sure to understand the history of anxiety precipitating these thoughts and feelings and therefore be able to utilize objectives to manage and control the underlying anxiety, aiming to prevent suicidal ideations or the intent to act on these thoughts.

One misconception about anxiety and depression that I hear all the time, whether it be a presentation on mental health or stress management or even from other treatment providers, is that anxiety and depression are two separate things. Anxiety and depression are *not* separate or unrelated. Depression is actually a continuum of the anxiety scale.

Depression results when we have already been battling high levels of anxiety for a prolonged period of time. When we find ourselves toward the top of the scale (around an 8, 9, or 10), it is extremely uncomfortable and overwhelming. We spend an exorbitant amount of energy—physically, mentally, and emotionally—when we are fighting high levels of anxiety. Although most people are not aware of what is happening with their anxiety and lack of control, we do know what it feels like to be completely overwhelmed.

We can't stay at the top of the scale for a prolonged period of time. We need to have some kind of relief on that scale. When we don't get a sense of relief and have been living at the top of the scale for a significant period of time, we eventually hit a wall, and we can't keep fighting the anxiety. To provide more context of this, think of drinking caffeine all day and all night. You are wide awake, going, going, going without any sleep. But we can't live without sleep. Eventually, our bodies are going to physically crash and burn. The same thing happens mentally when we are at the top of the scale for a prolonged period of time. We just can't live up there. We mentally crash and burn.

After being at the top of the scale for such a long time, week after week, month after month, year after year, the anxiety has physically, mentally, and emotionally wiped us out. We feel like we hit a wall. We start to feel like we don't care about certain things anymore. We start to lose interest or pleasure in things we used to enjoy. We have no more motivation to keep doing what we've been doing on a daily basis. We feel like we *just don't care*. This is where depression comes into play. Depression is a continuum of the scale. We have been sitting at the top of the scale, fighting the anxiety day in and day out, for weeks, months, or years on end, and we can't keep doing it. We are wiped out. We are completely overwhelmed. The anxiety has taken everything out of us. We feel like we've lost all control and don't know what to do anymore, and we don't see a way out of it. We feel helpless that we can do anything to make this feeling go away and feel hopeless that we will ever get out of this place. We've tried everything we possibly can to get out of this depression, and nothing has worked. We're helpless and hopeless.

Here is where we are highly vulnerable to engaging in self-destructive behaviors. We have been at the top of the scale for too long; we haven't had any relief; we are physically, mentally, and emotionally drained; and we don't know what to do. We've lost all control. We are *desperate* to find some kind of relief. What happens when we are in this state of depression for a significant period of time? We have tried everything we can possibly think of to get out of this depression, and nothing has worked. Again, we feel helpless and hopeless.

- Then we start to think, "Is this what my life is going to be like from here on out? This sucks."
- We start to think about what it would be like to not live like this anymore.
- We think about the relief if we weren't here anymore.
- We think about what is wrong with us when everyone around us is so damn happy while we can't remember the last time we even smiled.
- We question if we are going to feel this way for the rest of our lives, and, if so, can we *actually* live this way from here on out without experiencing any kind of positive emotion?
- We might think, "I would rather not wake up tomorrow than to feel this way for the rest of my life, but I don't see any way out of it."

Are you starting to understand how someone might start to have suicidal thoughts?

Those who have serious thoughts of suicide, meaning that they have a plan and are intent on acting on this plan, are likely *not* going to tell anyone they have these thoughts or plans. I often see or hear that this is a myth about suicide; however, this is *not* a myth. If someone intends on acting on their plan, they don't want to be stopped. When someone speaks about having suicidal ideations, as much as we don't want them to feel this way or to have these thoughts, we *want* them to tell us that they have these thoughts. It's an indication that they feel stuck and helpless and don't know what to do. It's common to hear people say, after someone close to them has committed suicide, that they recently spoke to them, and they seemed completely fine or happy. There was nothing to indicate that they were having a hard time. This is very common. It is not a myth. I've also experienced clients who have had intentions of acting on a plan and denied at the time of our session that they had suicidal thoughts or plans. Only after they came close to following through with their plan did they acknowledge what they had done.

I once spoke with an emergency room psychiatrist regarding one of my patients, who had been hospitalized for having suicidal ideations. Our patient had informed the psychiatrist that we were working on her anxiety, and the psychiatrist proceeded to tell me, "It's very rare to have someone with depression who also has anxiety." The psychiatrist was treating anxiety and depression as two separate things and did not understand that depression is a direct result of anxiety. Someone who is depressed may not look particularly anxious because they have been experiencing heightened anxiety for a prolonged period of time to the point where they can't fight the overwhelming feeling anymore. At this point, the patient has already hit that wall where they feel completely wiped out physically, mentally, and emotionally. They are not necessarily going to present as being "anxious."

This is a significant misunderstanding, by a psychiatrist no less, who does not understand how anxiety works. This is a problem. My client was not allowed to return to school until this psychiatrist approved of her going back. Yet the psychiatrist had no understanding of my patient's history of anxiety and how her anxiety affected her or even how she understood her own anxiety. He was strictly basing his diagnoses on how our patient was presenting at face value. Both the school and the psychiatrist failed to assess our patient accurately, and she was misdiagnosed in the hospital based on the psychiatrist's assumptions and his not understanding anxiety. I want to reiterate that this is a problem. We all need to be educated about anxiety and how it precipitates depression and suicidal thoughts. They are *not* unrelated.

When I'm working with clients who have reported feeling depressed or suicidal, my work is not focused on treating the depressive symptoms themselves. My focus is on addressing the root cause of the depressive symptoms, which is the anxiety. I will track the depressive symptoms and use them as mile markers because we obviously want the symptoms to decrease in frequency, intensity, and duration, but I'm not treating the actual symptoms. By tackling the root cause of the depression, the depressive symptoms will subside. If I strictly focus on treating the depressive symptoms and not treating the root cause of the depression, I would only be putting a Band-Aid over those symptoms. We can suppress certain symptoms, but if we aren't treating the cause of the symptoms, then the anxiety will manifest itself another way. However, by understanding how specific structures in the brain are weakened or dysregulated due to anxiety, clients can start to focus on specific brain strengthening exercises to help manage depression, along with their anxiety.

Think of the game Whac-A-Mole. When you hit one of the moles back into the hole, a mole will pop up somewhere else. Then you try to hit that mole, and another one pops up. The same thing happens with anxiety when it's not treated appropriately. We can work to eliminate certain symptoms of anxiety, but unless we understand what is causing the symptoms and get control over the core anxiety, we are just going to experience other symptoms of anxiety. If anger is one way in which our anxiety is manifested, we can consciously make an effort not to express our anger in such an aggressive manner. But again, if we're not addressing the root cause of our anger, we could start to develop a tic or start to experience gastrointestinal issues. No matter what the symptoms are, they won't completely go away if all we focus on is the symptoms themselves. If we treat the underlying cause of the symptoms—the anxiety—then the symptoms will actually start to subside.

According to the Centers for Disease Control and Prevention (2018), there has been a 30 percent increase in the suicide rate across the United States, averaging across all ages, since 1999. Furthermore, a study done by researchers at Yale University found that bullying victims are between two and nine times more likely to consider suicide than nonvictims (Yale University Study, 2008). Unfortunately, the suggestions provided by the CDC to help prevent suicide are minimal. None of these suggestions include trying to understand what precipitates someone contemplating suicide. The listed warning signs presented by the CDC do not address the role of a person's sense of control, or lack thereof, and do not assess anxiety. Again, anxiety is severely misunderstood, misdiagnosed, and mistreated.

Defense Mechanisms

What happens when we are not aware of anxiety or don't know appropriate ways to help ourselves feel better in those moments of stress? When we are not aware of our anxiety or how it is affecting us in the moment, we are likely to become defensive. We are more likely to react impulsively or irrationally or engage in some kind of avoidant behavior. This is when the amygdala receives information from the insula and hippocampus that tells it to activate the SRS because our sense of control is threatened. Our defenses are natural reactions when we feel threatened, when things don't go the way we want, or under any circumstance when we feel a lack of control. Our brain quickly interprets the situation as unsafe. It's our body's natural fight-or-flight response. We try to tackle the situation at hand by exercising control, albeit often in inappropriate or maladaptive ways, or we often avoid dealing with the anxiety-provoking situation. Using the scale from 0 to 10, when our anxiety is higher on the scale, around an 8, 9, or 10, we tend to have a very difficult time focusing, concentrating, or thinking rationally. Again, the SRS is activated, and the amygdala has sent a signal to slow or shut down the PFC, minimizing our ability to focus, problem-solve, or think rationally. Because we have a harder time thinking clearly when our anxiety is higher, we are more vulnerable to engaging in maladaptive behaviors that tend to be more impulsive or provide us with an immediate sense of relief, particularly when we are not aware of our anxiety and therefore do not know how to control it in a healthy manner. Even if we do not understand our anxiety, we know how we feel when we are at the top of the scale. We are well aware of the fact that we do not feel good and that it's too much to handle. At this point, if we are not aware of appropriate or healthy ways to help ourselves feel better when consumed with overwhelming anxiety, we are going to look for whatever is at our fingertips to help us feel better. More often than not, we will engage in maladaptive behavior. These maladaptive behaviors, which are outlined below, help bring an immediate sense of relief. Our anxiety goes down on the scale. While these maladaptive behaviors only bring temporary relief or a false sense of control, we still choose to engage in them for a "time out" from the anxiety, rather than sitting with that overwhelming feeling with no relief in sight.

For example, if we know that smoking marijuana will help us feel better almost immediately and decrease our anxiety, then there is a pretty good chance that we will continue to utilize the same resource the next time we're feeling highly anxious. We might come down on the scale rather quickly, but this will only last temporarily, and our actual level of control will stay very low. We're not doing anything to help manage the stressor that triggered our anxiety in the first place. We're going to keep going up and down on the scale, in a repetitive pattern, until we are able to break out of that cycle and find a more permanent way of managing our anxiety, ultimately gaining a greater, healthier, and more productive use of control.

Unfortunately, it can be very difficult to break this cycle. When we use marijuana, we feel better. It works. Why wouldn't we continue to use it to help ourselves feel better? It's much easier than taking the time to work on raising our sense of control. When we find something that works, which brings our anxiety down and makes us feel good, we are at a higher risk of continuing that behavior, even if it is not effective in the long run.

Now let's address what the neurotransmitters dopamine, norepinephrine, and serotonin do in this process. When we engage in a behavior that elicits a positive feeling, or what Dr. Stixrud refers to as a "reward," the level of dopamine in our system increases. Higher levels of dopamine allow us to feel better and act as a motivator to engage in certain behaviors. We're going to be more motivated to engage in a certain behavior if we know it will make us feel better. Just as higher levels of dopamine are associated with increased drive, according to Dr. Stixrud, lower levels of dopamine are associated with lower drive or minimal motivation, as well as boredom. Dr. Stixrud states that there needs to be an optimal level of dopamine in order for there to be a healthy flow for optimal functioning.

We can see a pattern of losing control or not having the level of control or sense of safety or security that we need when we look at significant life-altering experiences. These significant or traumatic life experiences can form negative core beliefs, especially in those of younger ages, making them more vulnerable to living with a heightened level of anxiety throughout their development and into adulthood. These experiences may include, but are not limited to:

- Loss

- Being bullied

- Abuse: verbal, physical, or sexual

- Neglect: physical or emotional

- Witnessing abuse of any kind

- Experiencing racism

- Not feeling they are living up to others' expectations

- Feeling like a failure

- Divorce or parents going through a divorce

- Losing a home due to various circumstances

- Constantly being compared to others

- Feeling unnoticed/not validated

- Having an alcoholic parent

- Having a family member in jail

- Being involved in the juvenile justice system

- Abandonment or forced separation

- Being in foster care

- Witnessing violence

- Experiencing war

- Seeking asylum

Unfortunately, these examples are only a handful of the significant life events that people can experience. However, all these situations are examples of when a person has limited to no sense of control. These are circumstances that are thrust upon them by someone/something else. No one chooses to be put in these situations. It's not just the actual events that can have a significant impact on a person; the way in which the person interprets or experiences an event can be additionally damaging. This becomes their mental "narrative" of their life and their view of themselves in their life story. For example, a child might assume that they are unlovable or a burden on their family or others, and that's why they are abused. They might internalize the belief that they deserve to be abused and don't deserve to be treated any differently in future relationships.

Loss is a significant example in which there is a substantial drop in our personal sense of control, whether it be death, a divorce, personal trauma such as losing a house in a fire or flood or losing a pet. These are all examples of significant loss that we do not choose to have happen. Unfortunately, we are left with trying to figure out how to get to a point of acceptance, after having emotionally processed our significant loss, and learning how to move forward in our lives. We have to learn what we can do for ourselves moving forward by focusing on the options that are within our control. Grieving helps us move through this process. We initially experience a state of denial, where we logically understand what has happened, but it is too much for us to emotionally process right away. Our brain needs time to think through and process the event, eventually making way for us to emotionally process that loss. Our emotions are all over the place, going through feelings of denial, anger, bargaining, and depression before finally getting to a place of acceptance.

According to the CDC (2018), a study that collected data from 2011 to 2012 found that children who were currently experiencing anxiety or depression were more likely than those not experiencing depression to have one or more of the following:

- Another mental, behavioral, or developmental disorder, such as ADHD, a learning disability, or speech or language problems

- Other chronic health conditions including gastrointestinal issues, autoimmune disorders, and even cancer (Mate, 2021; van der Kolk, 2015)

- School problems

- Parents who reported high levels of stress (their own anxiety) and frustration with parenting; and

- Unmet medical and mental health needs.

If a child is experiencing any of these issues, where is their sense of control likely to be? Their sense of control is going to be lower when they are not receiving support or care for medical or mental health issues. Their sense of control is going to be lower when they have parents who have high anxiety and unpredictable behavior. Their sense of control is going to be lower when they don't know how to successfully manage school problems or when they have a learning disorder, making it difficult for them to understand the material. When kids have a hard time understanding, sustaining attention, or listening, they are not going to feel they have a good sense of control in those circumstances, making them vulnerable to assuming negative thoughts about themselves that they aren't smart, will always be less than others, are a failure, et cetera. Chronic health problems prevent kids from being able to engage in routine daily activities, again limiting what they can do and their sense of control.

See a pattern here? It's understandable that if a child is struggling to learn material in school in the same capacity as other students, they are not going to feel they have control over their learning or academics if they are not able to meet the same expectations as their peers. This then leads students to start to feel like they aren't smart, or at least not as smart as their classmates, and they start to internalize these negative beliefs about themselves, affecting their core beliefs and self-esteem. If a child doesn't know how to get the support they need, again, they are not going to feel like they have control over their stressor and will likely not learn to focus on themselves versus comparing themselves to their peers.

Unfortunately, our defenses can become more harmful than helpful in the long-term. As our brain goes into survival mode when we first experience trauma or stressful circumstances that trigger our anxiety, our brain is doing exactly what it needs to do in that moment to keep us as safe as possible and alive. Our initial defense mechanisms can be lifesaving. Our defense mechanisms are also extremely adaptive. Once we engage in a defense mechanism that served us well and kept us safe and alive, our brain will automatically continue to engage in that defense mechanism when experiencing future anxiety or threats to our safety. This is where our defense mechanism may start to be more maladaptive than protective. Defense mechanisms are helpful and life-saving in the moment, but without processing the anxiety or trauma, the brain starts to function in maladaptive ways. That is why with Control Theory, along with working through the body to change the brain, Cognitive Behavioral Theory, and neuropsychological mental health education, we are trying to train our brains to think in a more logical step-by-step manner. We are teaching our brains to think differently than we have been used to thinking throughout our development and into adulthood, and helping our brains recover from the damage done from chronic anxiety and trauma. We are building new, healthier, adaptive neural networks, allowing us to live with past anxious thoughts without becoming overcome by them. When we can think in a more logical, step-by-step manner, we are better able to focus on what we need to do in the moment and what our priorities are, identify options that are within our control, and problem-solve more effectively.

Understanding Avoidance

At the cognitive level (versus instinctual fight, flight, or freeze responses), avoidance is one of the most common natural defense mechanisms. It makes sense. Why would we want to face an anxiety-provoking situation if we didn't have to, right? Avoidance will alleviate our anxiety in the moment, but it's only temporary, similar to other defense mechanisms or maladaptive behaviors. It is not a means of exercising control in a healthy or effective manner; rather, it provides a false sense of control. The anxiety will eventually increase again, oftentimes becoming higher than it was initially, and our sense of control stays very low on the scale. We don't actually gain control over the situation when we avoid it, and we then anticipate having to avoid it in the future. Until we understand why we feel anxious, confront the stressor, and identify what we can do to get some sense of control back, the anxiety will remain. When we avoid, we are putting off having to deal with the stressor, but that anxiety will still linger until we feel we have a greater sense of real power to change the situation.

Unfortunately, it is much easier to avoid a stressor in the moment than to confront the situation. When we are forced to deal with a provoking situation, we are likely to automatically assume the worst is going to happen and feel that we don't have the level of control we want or need in the moment. If we felt that we had everything under control and that things were happening predictably or as planned, then we would not be experiencing high anxiety. However, in the moment of stress and not feeling like we have full ability to shape a situation's outcome, we are prone to assume that we won't know what to do or how to handle the situation. It can be difficult to focus in the moment or shift our focus to what is within our control.

When our anxiety is high on the scale, and we are feeling extremely overwhelmed, avoidant behaviors can quickly bring some relief to that uncomfortable feeling. We can quickly lower our anxiety on the scale by avoiding an anxiety-provoking situation, whether it is happening in the moment, or we are anticipating having to deal with a stressful situation. For example, if a student experiences high anxiety when at school, it's common for them to try to avoid going to school. They may feel sick (not just claim to be sick but actually feel sick as a symptom of anxiety). They might experience anxiety or panic attacks when going to school or even thinking about going to school. If students are not educated about anxiety, including how their brain functions under anxiety, and are not taught to identify options that are within their control to manage the stressful situation appropriately and effectively at school, they are likely to engage in avoidant behaviors.

As students avoid school, it becomes harder for them to return. The longer they avoid it, the worse the anxiety gets. They start to become more dependent on their avoidance of school in an effort to manage their anxiety; however, they aren't getting any actual control over their anxiety. A student will likely feel temporary relief from their anxiety when they make the decision to skip school that day, but that anxiety is likely to return later that evening when the student knows they have to return to school the next day or the next morning when they are waking up or getting ready for school. Although some students may be well aware of why they don't want to go to school, they often don't know how to manage the stressor that is triggering their tension/fear. If they don't know what to do to manage the stressor—be it a test, a bully, social stressors, et cetera—they are not going to feel they have a good sense of control, which heightens their anxiety, making them want to avoid the situation altogether and retreat to their comfort zone or safe space.

Oftentimes, schools will have a tutor come to the student's home when they have not been able to return to school. But having a tutor come to the student's home is actually enabling the student's avoidant behavior and essentially increasing their anxiety. The student is not learning how to appropriately manage their anxiety and regain control and confidence. They are not learning how to manage the stressors at school that are triggering their anxiety. They are allowing these stressors to have control over them. The next time they experience similar events, they are not going to know what to do or how to handle the situation. Their immediate response when presented with similar circumstances is likely to be avoiding the situation and default to their "cop-out" solution. Until they understand their anxiety and learn appropriate ways to manage it and understand how to gain control over the stressor, their anxiety will continue to return, inhibiting their ability to engage in various situations or perform in more optimal ways.

Another example of avoidance as a defensive reaction is behaviors stemming from a fear of abandonment. Recall from our discussion about core beliefs that if a child is placed in the care of another who was not their initial caretaker, especially if they had already established a firm attachment with their initial caregiver, the child may then anticipate being abandoned by other caretakers or by others with whom they try to establish a relationship throughout their development and adulthood. Attachment also lays the foundation for feelings of containment and safety, or lack thereof. It is common for a child who has experienced people coming into their lives and then leaving at some point to assume that they will be abandoned by others. They are likely to have a difficult time allowing themselves to fully engage in a relationship (romantic, friendship, or otherwise) without anticipating the other person leaving them. The child, even as they develop into adulthood, is likely to push people away or detach themselves if they feel they are getting too close to someone and would be hurt by losing that person. When the child creates a barrier with another person, preventing them from getting emotionally close to that person, the child is able to exercise a sense of control to prevent getting hurt again. In other words, they can avoid experiencing another personal reaction and loss of their own sense of control.

Lastly, let's review the example from earlier in the book about Katie, my client who was able to recognize that her panic attack was caused by hearing the word *suicide* in one of her classes, even though the attack didn't occur until the end of the day when she was sitting down, relaxing. This is also an example of how avoiding processing an anxiety-provoking event, intentional avoidance or not, does not relieve the stress. Until we can understand the source, and therefore identify what we can do that's within our control, we cannot manage anxiety-provoking situations. Avoidant "coping skills" will only help alleviate our anxiety temporarily. They won't prevent the anxiety from continuing to affect us, and we aren't finding the source of the anxiety by just using coping skills. These skills can help calm us when our anxiety is high on the scale, but once we've come down to where we can think more logically, we need to utilize cognitive objectives to address the cause of the anxiety, giving us more insight and, therefore, a better understanding of how to control it. As previously stated, when we avoid having to deal with the stressor, that anxiety will linger until we feel we have a greater sense of control over the situation.

Substance Use and Self-Harm

Substance use is another example of avoidant behavior. When our anxiety is high on the scale and we are feeling overwhelmed, we are going to look for the fastest and easiest way to alleviate our anxiety if we don't have the awareness or education on ways to exercise healthy control.

Let's go back to the example of a student experiencing high anxiety at school. Avoiding school may or may not be the primary choice to alleviate the student's anxiety. Students might choose alternate routes to avoid dealing with their stressors. If alcohol and drugs are easily accessible, there's a good chance that students will think about using substances. If they choose to use drugs or alcohol when feeling highly anxious or stressed, they will feel their anxiety decrease rather quickly.

Unfortunately, drugs and alcohol do often work in the short

term. If we have a drink, or two, or more, we can numb uncomfortable feelings. We can bring ourselves down on the anxiety scale and feel a temporary sense of relief. We might actually feel pseudo happy for a short amount of time, feeling a false sense of control. If we smoke marijuana, our anxiety will go down. If we take some prescription pills, we can try to numb our worries. Self-harm, such as cutting, can also bring that quick sense of relief by distracting us from our emotional pain with physical sensations. Self-harm is not only a defense mechanism, but it is also a way in which the cingulate brings someone back to the present moment when they are emotionally detached from what is happening to them or dissociating. People who dissociate will often engage in self-harm to bring them back to the present moment. Dissociation results from trauma. By dissociating, we cut ourselves off from overwhelming experiences and feelings. Memories become fragmented and we keep reliving past experiences because sensory information from the memory intrudes into the present, where they are literally being relived as flashbacks. The hippocampus is not able to provide clear context, but only fragmented information. As the trauma networks continue to be activated, they become stronger, and the cingulate becomes weakened. Self-harm, such as cutting, is one mechanism that activates the cingulate to refocus back to the present.

What happens when that temporary relief starts to go away? Our anxiety goes right back up on the scale, oftentimes worse than it was before we engaged in the maladaptive behavior. The next time we start to feel that overwhelming anxiety again and we don't have the proper tools or awareness to know how to manage it, we are going to use what worked before, again, and again, and again. It works, right? So why wouldn't we do it again? When we continue to go back to using or relapse, the amygdala is connected to a reward circuit in the brain. This reward circuit reinforces the addiction (Sweeton, 2019). Thrill seekers also have strong insulas that are hooked into the reward circuits. With dissociation, the insula is turned off, and the cingulate, which is also part of the "here and now" network and connects you to yourself and your environment, turns off during dissociation. Unfortunately, with self-harm, the insula and cingulate become activated to bring the person back to the present, which is what we need, to bring our focus back to the present, but we need to have other options to tap into the insula (which we will discuss later).

Here is where we get caught in a trap where our anxiety comes down temporarily when we find something that works to alleviate that awful feeling, but then the anxiety soon returns to the higher level on the scale. We get trapped in a cycle of dependence on the maladaptive behavior that helped bring us relief, even if it was temporary. We become dependent on these maladaptive behaviors to help ourselves feel better when we don't have adequate awareness about our anxiety and don't know appropriate ways in which we can control it. However, the "relief" becomes less effective over time and repeated use of this crutch as the problems of the real world are banging down the door. You can't avoid them forever.

But that's just it—it's temporary. The use of a substance or self-destructive behavior will only temporarily bring relief from the anxiety, bringing us a false sense of control. Our actual level of control is still minimal. We are not gaining any control over the anxiety or overwhelming feelings by depending on a substance to alleviate that awful feeling. But because it works, usually very quickly, and this is all we know to alleviate the anxiety, we are at risk of developing a dependence on a substance or a behavior in an effort to manage our overwhelming anxiety. We have not gained any control over our anxiety (or the source of the anxiety) by engaging in these behaviors. We may feel like we are on top of the world for a bit, but then we start to feel powerless, desperate, and disgusted with ourselves. The root cause of that anxiety still needs to be identified and addressed.

Other Avoidant Behaviors

Other avoidant behaviors that we might experience or witness are lying, manipulation, blaming others for our actions, and justifying or making excuses for our wrongful actions or choices. These avoidant behaviors are examples of not taking accountability for our decisions.

Lying

An example of lying as an avoidant defense mechanism is if a child, Jimmy, hits a friend, Thomas, and Thomas runs to his parents to tell them what Jimmy did. Jimmy will quickly feel an increase in his anxiety. Granted, children are typically not aware of anxiety, nor do they understand this abstract concept. However, they are well aware of their uncomfortable feelings even if they can't verbalize them. If Jimmy is afraid of getting in trouble, his anxiety is going to be higher on the scale. Usually, kids don't like to get in trouble. If Jimmy is anticipating that he will get in trouble (an example of an automatic thought without having evidence it will happen), then Jimmy might assume his parents will be very angry with him. If his parents are angry with him, he won't be able to keep playing. He will have to go to his room, he will miss out on something or not be able to play with Thomas or his other friends, his friends will think he's not a good kid, they will make fun of him . . . and on and on his thoughts will spiral.

What does a child do when he's consumed by these automatic thoughts? Naturally, he will likely go into defense mode. He's thinking of the fastest solution to prevent getting in trouble or upsetting his parents. The first thing Jimmy might think of in that moment is to lie to his parents and say he didn't hit Thomas. He might think that if he lies, he will avoid getting in trouble. He will avoid the embarrassment of admitting he acted inappropriately. Let's say Jimmy lies to his parents, and his parents believe his lie. In that moment, Jimmy's anxiety drops dramatically on the scale. He feels a big sense of relief because he avoided getting in trouble. He avoided his parents getting mad at him. He avoided losing playtime or time with his friends. He avoided being embarrassed. He also avoided taking personal responsibility for his actions. What did Jimmy learn from that experience? If he's afraid of getting in trouble in the future, he can lie again so he doesn't get in trouble. He doesn't learn how to take accountability. If lying worked for him, there's a good chance that he's going to do it again if he's in a stressful situation where he is being held accountable for something and doesn't want to get in trouble.

If we don't learn how to take ownership of our actions when we are younger, we will continue to engage in the same maladaptive behaviors or find other avoidant maladaptive behaviors to use each time our anxiety spikes as we continue throughout our development and even into adulthood. If our immediate gut reaction is to lie or place blame on others throughout our development and we aren't taught about the importance of accountability, then, as adults, we are going to do the same thing. We need to teach our children appropriate and healthy ways to manage stressful situations, especially when they are at fault, or their actions will translate to real-world issues. Furthermore, parents need to react appropriately so their kids aren't scared to tell the truth and to communicate that lying may be worse than the actual behavior.

Now let's think about what these defense mechanisms turn into as we get older. What do these behaviors look like in adults when we aren't taught how to appropriately manage our anxieties? Adults who never learned how to take accountability for their actions are likely to justify their behaviors (to themselves and to others), make excuses for why they did what they did, blame others for their mistakes, or manipulate others to do what they want or take the blame. They will experience temporary relief of anxiety in the moment if they can blame someone else or "justify" their actions, convincing themselves that what they did wasn't really that bad or that they themselves are really not at fault. But they know what they did was not right, and they will continue to lie to cover previous lies or work even harder to convince others that they aren't wrong. This sounds stressful and tiring!

Let's go back to the example of Jimmy and Thomas. Why did Jimmy hit Thomas in the first place? What was the purpose of that behavior? It might have been his way of trying to control Thomas. Jimmy may not have liked the fact that he wasn't getting what he wanted from Thomas. When we engage in aggressive behaviors, it is often a defensive response. We might be trying to get something we want or to exercise control over others in order to get them to do what we want. We are also struggling to accept that we don't have control of what is happening in that circumstance or that we don't have control over another person. We don't want to accept that we are not getting what we want. When we have a hard time accepting that we don't have control over others or various circumstances, we often try to exert control in other ways or up the ante and put pressure on others to get what we want. This leads us to our next topic: manipulation.

Manipulation

Manipulation is another example of how we act in order to exert control over others to try and get what we want. It's common to engage in manipulative behavior when our anxiety is high, and we don't want to accept what is not within our control or take accountability for our own actions. If a child wants something, such as a toy that another child is playing with, they may or may not understand that they have to wait their turn. Also, kids often do not want to wait their turn. They also don't like to hear the word *no*. When they are told no or that they can't have what they want, they are going to up the ante in order to get what they want. They might yell, bite, hit, et cetera. Kids have a hard time accepting what is not within their control because, in many cases, they don't have much control. They want what they want when they want it. If they can't get what they want, they try whatever it takes to convince others to give them what they want.

Kids are master manipulators. It's a natural defense mechanism for them as they are trying to figure things out in the world. They are trying to learn what they are able to do, what they can't do, and what they're not allowed to do. Manipulation is part of a child's development. They will come up with every possible reason they should be allowed to have what they want. They just don't want to accept the answer no. Again, kids do not like to accept what is not within their control. When they are not getting what they want, they quickly become frustrated or angry. In other words, they become anxious. They feel anxious in that moment when they aren't getting what they want. Although kids don't exercise this level of conscious, abstract thinking, they are no less prone to reacting, often in inappropriate ways, when they don't have the level of control that they want or need.

Another way in which kids can manipulate us to get what they want is by splitting their parents. Oftentimes, kids will ask one parent for something, and when that parent says no, they will go ask the other parent. The child (usually) won't mention that they already asked the other parent. They will just try a new tactic with the second parent.

Here's an example from when I was about eight years old. My parents owned a business in our town, and right around the corner from our family's business was a grocery store. I was hanging out at our business one day and went over to the grocery store. In front of the grocery store were some girls with a box of puppies, giving the puppies away. I really wanted a puppy. My mom came over to the store. (I'm not sure if she was actually looking for me, but let's pretend she was.) She saw me with the puppies. I asked her if we could have one. She said no. Now, my parents are animal lovers, and we already had a dog, so I really didn't think it was a big deal as a kid. I started to beg and plead. She told me to go ask my dad. "If your dad says yes, then I'll say yes."

I was so excited! I brought a puppy over to my dad at work and asked him if we could keep it. He asked me what my mom said. I told him, "She said yes!" I purposely left out the part where she said, "*If* your dad says yes." I remember thinking that I wasn't being totally honest, but in my mind, I wasn't completely lying either. I was justifying my actions and what I told my dad in my head. Since my dad was under the impression that my mom had already made the decision and said yes, he said yes.

I ran back to the store to find my mom and told her that my dad said yes. (He did!) Later that night, when my parents were home, I found out that they had a discussion about the dog. I'm not sure how the conversation went exactly, but it was along the lines of:

"I didn't say she could have a dog."

"She said you said yes."

"I didn't say yes. I said, I'd say yes if you said yes."

"Well, she told me that you said yes."

So, in summary, I didn't like the first answer I got from my mom, I upped the ante and guilted her; I manipulated my parents and our conversations, they didn't communicate with each other in the meantime, and I got a new puppy. I found a way to get what I wanted.

There are exceptions for babies or children with special needs when reacting to various situations when their behaviors aren't necessarily manipulative. Babies will cry when they are hungry, tired, or in pain. They aren't being manipulative, but they are communicating that their needs are not entirely met, and they are not happy. Essentially, they don't have the level of control they need in a particular situation, albeit in a more primitive form. However, as they get older, we still have to set limits with them and communicate to them in a such a way that they understand that they are not always going to get what they want, such as watching television all day or eating cookies whenever they want. We have to start teaching them about the word *no* very early to facilitate their ability to accept when they are told no throughout their development.

Children with special needs might also escalate their behaviors if they feel their needs are not being met or if they are feeling completely overwhelmed or overstimulated in their environment. They may not be trying to manipulate a situation when their behavior escalates physically, but they are still communicating that they don't feel in control, and it's too much. They need help communicating effectively when they don't have the skills to do so yet, and we need to be mindful of this. Communication (which will be further discussed later in the reading) is key for each and every person to feel they have a greater sense of control.

Bullying

Another example of how kids can utilize these interpersonal

skills is when they are bullied. When a child is taught interpersonal/communication skills, they will be more prepared when another child tries to overpower or emotionally damage them. We want our kids to know how to maintain their own sense of self and self-control. We want them to understand that no other kids can control them while, at the same time, they can't control other kids. They are in control of themselves.

If a child is being bullied, we want them to know that they can set a limit with the bully or aggressor and hold them accountable. Initially, if a child is being bullied, their anxiety is going to quickly increase. They will (we hope only momentarily) feel a loss in control when another child is overpowering them and trying to control them through physical violence, humiliation, ostracizing, or other emotional abuse or manipulation. When a child experiences this power dynamic, we want them to be able to recognize it. We want them to have a fundamental understanding that it is not OK for others to control them in an aggressive or manipulative way.

One of the most important words we can teach our kids is no. When a child is being bullied, we want their automatic response to be "*No!*" This is one of the most important limits that a child can set. Just by telling their aggressor no, they are giving the bully the message that the bully cannot control them. They are telling the bully that they are in control of themselves and do not have to do what the bully tells them to do or allow the bully to make them feel bad about themselves in any way. We need to teach our children the importance of this word, not just for protecting themselves, but also in the context that if we choose not to respect someone else telling us no, that we are choosing to have the consequences.

Kids, as well as adults, need to understand how critical the word *no* is, no matter the circumstance. Kids need to learn that they cannot control other kids or intentionally hurt them or make them feel bad without repercussions. If they choose to act in any of these ways, they will be held accountable, and there will be consequences for those actions. The word *no* also teaches kids about accepting what is not in their control. We all have to understand that we can't have control over everything or over other people. What we do have control over is ourselves and the way in which we can communicate in order to get things done, get the help we need, or hold others accountable.

Although the word *no* has power to it, there is oftentimes a concern as to why people often struggle to say no. People often fear how others will react, that they will be humiliated, or that others will seek retaliation if we say no to them or hold them accountable in any way. We need to understand that it is critical for us to hold others accountable and to say no to them when they are crossing boundaries and harming others for the sake of getting what they want. We need to be able to focus on the fact that others are not entitled to have control over us in negative, harmful, or threatening ways. *We* are in control of ourselves, whether others like it or not.

When we don't say no to others and do not hold them accountable, we are allowing others to have control over us. We are giving them the message that what they are doing is OK. Even if we are anticipating how that person might react if we set a limit with them (although we don't have proof that they will definitely react in a negative way), we still need to set limits and hold them accountable. Again, if we are consistent in setting limits, eventually others will know what to expect from us. They can't have control over us. When we stop ourselves from setting limits because we are afraid of how the other person might react, we are giving them our control. Consistency in limit setting is critical.

There will still be times when saying no to someone might not work. This is actually typical when we haven't previously been setting limits with others, and we have (unintentionally) allowed others to overpower us in some capacity. When we start setting limits, what often happens is that the other person doesn't like the shift in control. When we set limits, we are giving them the message that they no longer have control over us and that we are in control of ourselves. This is often difficult for the aggressor to accept, at least initially. In addition to being consistent with setting limits and holding the bully accountable for their behavior, we can present a choice to them if they continue to not accept no as an answer: "If you choose not to respect my answer and continue disrespecting me, you are ultimately choosing to get a higher authority involved. That's not my choice. That's the choice you are making as you choose to continue these inappropriate behaviors."

You are not threatening the other person but are pointing out the fact that the situation will reach another level if they choose to continue acting in an aggressive manner. You are continuing to hold the person accountable by putting the responsibility for their behaviors on them. You are not going to take responsibility for their behaviors or continue to allow them to exercise control over you.

I started working with Shawn during the spring of his junior year in high school. Shawn is a very talented, smart, responsible young man. He's a very strong student, active in several sports, hardworking (he even earned his Eagle Scout Badge), and has many friends and some very good close friends. Shawn has always been respectful of others, has always had good relationships with his teachers and coaches, and has very strong relationships with his parents and sister. I started seeing Shawn when he was having a hard time with two of his [then] friends inside and outside of school. These were friends who Shawn has known since elementary school. They had been inseparable up until high school. As they started going through high school, Shawn became friends with other classmates, but remained good friends with his two buddies from childhood. He wouldn't exclude them to do anything, but rather try to include everyone when getting together. Over the course of a couple of years, Shawn's two friends started to treat Shawn disrespectfully. They would publicly humiliate him, and also took their behavior to social media. But that wasn't enough. They went on to blackmail Shawn in order to have control over him. As strong as Shawn was, he's also human and has a breaking point. He had become overwhelmingly anxious over the course of two years, to the point where he was significantly depressed. He was still able to go through his days, meeting his responsibilities, but the depression took hold of him. He was at a breaking point. This is when he started coming to therapy.

My work with Shawn focused on anxiety management. I didn't treat his depressive symptoms. I explained what anxiety is and that it is rooted in experiencing a lack of control. We took a deeper look into the ways in which his "friends" were exercising control over him. For whatever reason, they wanted to hurt him, emotionally. They wanted to cause him pain. They wanted to humiliate him. We don't know why they behaved in these ways or why they were out to get Shawn, but there's a good chance that they were struggling with their own sense of self and self-esteem. It's possible they were jealous of Shawn.

We also talked about if there was anything Shawn might have done to upset or frustrate them, but we weren't able to identify anything, which is consistent with his character. Shawn was able to give examples of when he's messed up and was able to take accountability for his actions. He didn't struggle to take ownership in his choices. This is an area I immediately explore with my clients. However, I did not find this to be an area of concern for Shawn. Given that he truly felt he did not do anything (at least intentionally) to hurt his friends, we shifted our focus to identify ways in which Shawn can start to take control back over his life and not allow others to have that hold on him anymore. We focused on the fact that his "friends" don't have control over him, but that he has control over himself. We focused on communication, setting limits with others that allowed Shawn to feel a greater sense of personal control while letting others know that they can't have control over him. We practiced holding others accountable for their behaviors and choices. We reiterated over and over again that they do not have control over Shawn, but that he has control over himself.

Shawn started to lay out choices for these two classmates. He let them know that if they chose to continue to threaten him, then they are choosing to get school authorities involved and are ultimately choosing to be given natural consequences for their choices. He let them know that they are choosing to lose a longtime friend and would continue to lose friends if they keep treating others the way they've treated Shawn. Shawn put the responsibility on them. He worked hard to take his control back. Shawn continuously held them accountable any time they started to cross a boundary, which reinstated every time that they did not control Shawn. He was in control of himself.

Within a matter of three months, Shawn gained tremendous insight to his own anxiety, as well as how it affects others, and was able to bring his anxiety levels down significantly. Because he tackled his anxiety, his depressive symptoms subsided. He was happy again. All of this work happened before the school year ended.

Fast-forward to the fall of Shawn's senior year in high school. Shawn was on the football team. He was in the locker room after practice one night, after most of his teammates left. There was one other teammate, an underclassman, sitting on the bench with his head down, crying. Shawn sat down next to him and asked what was wrong. His teammate opened up to Shawn and told him that he was being bullied. Shawn quickly empathized with him and told his teammate his own story. Shawn also told him that these other kids don't have control over him. He emphasized to his teammate that no one else has control over him, that he is in control of himself. Shawn continued to tell his teammate what he did to get his own personal control back when he was bullied. The key work he emphasized: control.

Later that evening, Shawn's mother received a phone call from that teammate's mother, thanking her and Shawn. It turns out that student who was crying on the locker room bench was planning on taking his own life that night. After Shawn took the time to sit and talk with him and hearing what Shawn had to say, he decided to not follow through with his plan. Imagine being told that. You helped save another student's life, or your own child helped save another student's life. The word *powerful* isn't strong enough to describe what happened. Imagine if we bring this education into schools, where everyone can work together to lift each other up, and who knows... save each other.

One other important example of understanding the word *no* is with regard to sexual harassment and assault. If we teach kids when they are young that they don't have control over others, and vice versa, as they get older, we can instill the message that control also refers to assaulting others. We want our kids to learn how to hold others accountable and continue to practice this throughout their lives. We want to help them be prepared to focus on ways in which they are in control and to hold others accountable for their actions if someone tries to exercise inappropriate control over them. In addition, we want our adolescents, young adults, and children to understand that they are not allowed to exercise harmful and inappropriate control over others and that they, too, will be held accountable for their actions. If they practice setting limits and holding others accountable for unhealthy or inappropriate choices, others around them will start to see this pattern and will know what to expect from our kids: that if someone chooses to control them inappropriately, they will be held accountable and will have consequences.

Violence and Aggression

Another defense mechanism can be manifested through aggressive or bullying behaviors. Bullying and aggressive behaviors are additional examples of how we can exercise a temporary (false) control when we feel we don't have the desired level of control in one or more aspects of our lives. It's much easier to project our anxiety onto others, make others feel less about themselves, and put our and others' attention onto others than to focus on ourselves and take accountability for our own behaviors. If we don't have a strong or positive sense of self, resulting from high anxiety, it's easier to exercise control over others than to acknowledge how we feel about ourselves. We don't want to acknowledge our vulnerabilities because we will likely interpret these vulnerabilities as weaknesses. Instead of focusing on what we need to do to take care of ourselves or taking accountability for our actions and choices, we can more easily exercise control over others and project our anxiety onto them. Therefore, we don't need to focus on ourselves. We convince ourselves that we're not the ones who are struggling, but it's everyone else who has the problem. They become scapegoats.

We are more likely to engage in violent or aggressive behaviors when we have already been battling high levels of anxiety for a prolonged period of time. That means we have been feeling a loss of control for a significant period of time and have a hard time or are unwilling to accept what is not within our control, where we then try to control others around us. We are at the top of the scale, having little to no relief on the scale and very little, if any, sense of control over significant areas of our lives. As previously discussed, when we are at the top of the scale for so long with no alleviation from the stress, we eventually hit a wall where we physically, mentally, and emotionally can't keep fighting the anxiety. We eventually start to feel helpless and hopeless after we try numerous things to help us feel better, and nothing works. It feels like this awful feeling will never end. This is also where depression comes into play, as mentioned earlier. We become desperate for control and want to end our suffering.

An example of this level of aggression and violence is mass shootings. The decision to engage in such a violent way is likely not an impulsive decision or reaction. We need to think about what warning signs there might be that can result in someone feeling the need to exert power over others to such a degree. What might that person have experienced where they continuously felt a loss of personal control? In addition to the previous list of life circumstances that limit our sense of control, we need to ask these important questions:

- Were they bullied as a child or throughout their development?

- Did they feel they weren't living up to others' expectations?

- Did they feel like a failure?

- Did they feel they were constantly compared to others?

- Were they feeling unnoticed/not validated?

When we have been experiencing these circumstances, especially over a prolonged period of time, the anxiety wipes us out, and we fall into a state of depression, leading to a state of helplessness and hopelessness. Not that we don't need to hold individuals accountable for creating mass destruction, but we also need to consider what precipitates a person acting in these ways, to empathize with them, and to understand how to help others who could potentially be in this state of despair. This doesn't mean we need to agree with the choices they make, and again, they need to be held accountable for their actions, but people don't get to this level of destruction for no reason. We need to get to the root of these patterns and educate those around us, especially our children and students, so we can all learn why we feel anxiety, where it comes from, and what our anxiety does to us and learn healthy ways of exercising control rather than engaging in maladaptive and destructive behaviors. (I will further address bullying when discussing communication.)

Aggression and violence are ways to avoid reflecting on our own needs and vulnerabilities. It's easier to justify to ourselves that others are responsible for where we are today and why we are struggling. However, here is where we want to work on identifying our core beliefs and shift our focus to what we can do for ourselves moving forward. For example, if we experienced being abused as children, we want to focus on where the power of control is. When we were children, our abusers exercised control over us. However, after recognizing this (and by working through the nervous system and body to help stabilize and manage the SRS), we are able to work on shifting that control back into our own hands, where we can hold our abusers accountable for their actions and what they did to us while recognizing that we are taking back our control. We can also hold others accountable if we ever feel taken advantage of or controlled. We need to know that we are in control of ourselves and not allow others to have control over us.

Communication

How do we work with others in an effective way, even if things aren't going the way we want? How do we get others to understand our perspectives, thoughts, worries, or concerns? How do we work with kids to help them learn how to make better choices and not act aggressively when they don't get what they want? How do we help kids stop others from bullying them? The answer: communication. The focus: control. When we communicate, we are exercising healthy and productive control, as well as helping establish a healthy sense of control for our kids. Feeling listened to changes the physiology of our brains (van der Kolk, 2015). Being able to articulate a complex feeling and having feelings recognized activates our limbic system (van der Kolk, 2015). Communication goes hand in hand with our visceral bodily sensation and awareness. Being able to perceive visceral sensations is the foundation to our emotional awareness. Recall that Dr. van der Kolk states that emotions are sensory. Pendulating between language and the body, between remembering the past and feeling alive in the present, allows us to work through our trauma. When used appropriately, communication is one of our most significant tools for exercising control and managing our anxiety. The following communication objectives can be applied to both kids and adults.

Validation, Setting Limits, and Providing Choices

Adriana was told to stop playing and clean up her toys because it's time to eat dinner. Adriana doesn't want to stop playing and doesn't do what she's told. Her mother continues to tell her to clean up, and Adriana continues not to listen or to do what she is told. Her mother's frustration (anxiety) increases as she feels Adriana is not listening to her. When a parent feels their child is not listening to them, they aren't going to feel like they have control over the situation; hence, the anxiety quickly increases.

While trying to convince Adriana that she needs to clean up, her mother might raise her voice as she's getting frustrated; this will increase Adriana's anxiety. By raising her voice, her mother is using a maladaptive approach to control Adriana and get her to do what she's told. If Adriana is being told to do something she doesn't want to do, her mother's frustration/anxiety increases as she feels she does not have the level of control that she wants in that moment, and Adriana will also feel as though she is being controlled to a greater extent as her mother continues to raise her voice.

How does the mother communicate with Adriana to get control of the situation? If Adriana starts to get upset because she doesn't want to stop playing, her mom can validate her feelings by letting her know that she understands Adriana doesn't want to stop playing, and she's allowed to feel mad that she has to clean up, but then set a limit by giving Adriana a choice. She can choose to do what she's told and clean up her mess so there won't be any consequences, or, if she chooses not to listen and not to clean up, then her mother will take her toys away, or she will lose playtime after dinner. The mother can validate her daughter's feelings, present the two options, and then ask, "What's your choice?" When her feelings are validated, Adriana's frustration/anxiety will likely start to come down even slightly because she is given the message that it's OK to feel upset, and there is nothing wrong with that feeling, even though it's not comfortable. Adriana will also feel like her mother is listening to her if her feelings are validated. Just like adults, when kids feel like they are listened to, their sense of control will increase, which automatically starts to decrease their anxiety. By providing Adriana with choices, her mother is setting boundaries and letting Adriana know that Mom is in charge, and Adriana can't always do what she wants. Adriana, therefore, learns how to accept when things don't go her way.

Parents need to be consistent with setting limits and following through in order for their child to learn how to accept when they don't have control over something and that not everything will go their way. At the same time, by giving the kids choices, they are still able to exercise control and decide how they want to handle the situation. Adriana can still make a good choice and not have a consequence. By asking Adriana, "What's your choice?" her mother transfers responsibility from the parent to the child. The question reiterates that it's Adriana's choice and her responsibility to handle the situation appropriately. If Adriana chooses not to make a good choice, she will essentially learn that she is accountable for her own actions and choice. The choice being made is not the mother's (and the mother doesn't want Adriana to get a negative consequence), but if Adriana decides to make a wrong choice, then she learns accountability (again with consistency from her mother setting limits). The mother can reiterate that Adriana made the choice not to clean up and therefore chose to have a consequence. It was not the mother's choice. Her mother can also reinforce that she has Adriana's best interest at heart and wants her to learn to recognize her responsibility in her decisions.

There is still a benefit to a child making the wrong choice as they start to learn the importance of accountability. Accountability is another significant tool to help decrease anxiety. As Adriana learns about accountability, she will also experience a decrease in her anxiety. Because she's taking ownership of her behaviors and choices, she learns to accept when she doesn't get her way and when she doesn't have control over a particular circumstance. Furthermore, by providing Adriana with choices, the mother exercises control over her own anxiety by not getting into a power struggle with her daughter. By transferring responsibility to Adriana, she is giving her daughter an opportunity to exercise control while still setting boundaries for her. Both Adriana and her mother are able to maintain control of their anxiety and have a better, healthier sense of control by communicating rather than engaging in an argument.

What happens when we don't communicate effectively? Think about when you are trying to talk to someone, and they talk over you, or they aren't paying attention. Do you feel like they are listening to you? Do you feel like you have control in the conversation when the other person isn't listening to you? If we don't feel we have control, our anxiety (frustration, anger, annoyance) automatically increases. What do we tend to do if someone isn't listening to us? We might raise our voices, or we might interrupt them. We do this as a reaction to not feeling the level of control we need in that moment. We are trying to exercise control over the other person; however, raising our voices or talking over them is not actually going to give us control. We will feel more of a false sense of control. In that moment, if we raise our voices, our anxiety might come down just slightly on the scale, but our actual sense of control stays very low. Our anxiety will quickly return to a higher level on the scale the second the other person raises their voice or interrupts us again. What starts to happen is that we get into a power struggle. If we raise our voices over the other person, they will likely do the same, and we keep getting louder and louder, interrupting each other and not listening to what the other is saying. We are both fighting for control, yet the conversation turns into an argument, and neither one of us has control. In fact, our sense of control keeps lowering the more we argue, which automatically increases our anxiety.

How do we maintain or exercise appropriate control in a stressful conversation? First, we need to practice listening. We may not necessarily like what we hear all the time, but we need to listen to others. By practicing listening, we are allowing the other person to communicate more effectively, even if they are more emotional in what they are saying. The person speaking is going to feel they have at least some control in the conversation if the other person is listening.

Once that person is done presenting what they have to say, they will likely allow us to have that same opportunity to express our concerns. This also teaches us to accept when others may not agree with us (accepting what is not within our control). Keep in mind, just because we are working on communicating effectively and appropriately, it does not mean that we always have to agree with the other person or have the same opinion or perspective. We are focusing strictly on the way in which we communicate.

Now, if we feel that another person is talking in a rude, inappropriate, or disrespectful way, we can still exercise appropriate control by setting a limit with that person: "If you continue to be disrespectful to me, I'm not going to engage in this conversation. If you choose to speak and act respectfully, then I will listen. It's up to you." This is an example of how we can set a limit and hold the other person accountable while maintaining appropriate control at the same time. We are not controlling the other person. We are giving them the message that we will not allow them to speak to us disrespectfully, that they don't have control over us, and that we are not doormats. If they still choose to be disrespectful, we can say, "You've made your choice. I'm not going to continue with this conversation. You can let me know when you are ready to have an appropriate conversation."

We can then walk away. We maintain control of ourselves. We don't allow the other person to have control over us. We hold the other person accountable while still allowing them an opportunity to resume the conversation if they choose to act appropriately. The more consistent we are with setting limits, holding others accountable, and following through with these limits, the more others will start to understand what to expect from us. They will understand that they can't control or manipulate us, but we won't shut them out either. They will understand that we are still willing to work with and talk with them, if they approach us respectfully.

Once each person has had an opportunity to present their concerns, we want to make sure that we understand each other. This is where we validate, or repeat back to the other person, what they said or how we understand they feel. When we receive validation, we again feel like the other person is listening to us, even if they don't agree with us. The main point is to listen and understand the other person's perspective. Again, we don't have to agree with them, but it is important to understand their perspective. If we repeat back to the other person what we understand from what they said and have completely misunderstood them, they then have an opportunity to correct us and clarify what they said.

This is an important step. If I'm listening to someone and I misinterpret what they are saying, I could very easily start to assume they mean something else, and my assumptions (automatic thoughts) will start snowballing, and then I'm jumping to conclusions, getting more and more frustrated (anxious). As I'm creating all these false assumptions in my head, I'm becoming more vulnerable to reacting irrationally and losing my temper and my sense of control. I can nip this reaction in the bud if I simply repeat back to the person what I thought they said. If I'm wrong, they can correct me and therefore prevent me from creating more assumptions in my head and losing control in the conversation. Keep in mind, it's our responsibility to communicate our assumptions or understanding of what was said to the other person.

This communication approach is effective for people of all ages. We can use these objectives when talking with other adults, teenagers, and even toddlers. Think about how toddlers react when they don't feel understood. We see more aggressive behaviors and meltdowns. As they learn how to communicate better and more effectively, those negative behaviors tend to decrease because they learn other ways to communicate where they feel they have more control. If we can teach our kids these communication tools, they will likely be able to communicate much more effectively throughout their development and as adults. They will be able to handle social situations more effectively. They will be able to set limits with others and hold others accountable when needed. These positive techniques and objectives are transferred to adulthood. If children are taught accountability when they are younger, they will be more likely to take accountability for their actions as they get older. They will therefore be able to manage their anxiety more effectively and be better skilled in relationships and many domains of life.

Self-Control

An example of how our children learn the importance of self-control is in the home. When a child is raised in a chaotic environment with limited structure or rules, they don't experience having a solid sense of control. When they are in a chaotic environment, they feel chaotic, just as a game without rules is chaos—the rules give the game meaning. At the other end of the spectrum, when kids are in a highly controlled environment with limited ability to explore and learn on their own, they will feel controlled, and their anxiety is already heightened. They are highly vulnerable to experiencing anxiety. They are likely not taught to self-regulate in a healthy manner and are less likely to have tools to help calm them. These environments increase the risk of kids engaging in defensive or maladaptive behaviors as a primary coping mechanism to alleviate their anxiety. They experience a lack of containment, which essentially inhibits their ability to feel safe.

We need to have a middle ground. When children are provided structure, routine, and rules, even if they don't like the rules, there is a feeling of safety and comfort. This safety comes from having a predictable routine with understandable rules and consequences, teaching them accountability, teaching them to accept when they don't have control over everything or over others, that not everything goes their way, and it's OK. If a child's environment is predictable, they are going to have a stronger sense of control and a better understanding of their own responsibilities. When anxiety is not dealt with at a young age, it then continues into adolescence and adulthood. This is where children tend to have a higher baseline level of anxiety (although they are unaware of it) and have a hard time self-regulating, communicating, or even creating their own daily or weekly structured routine, let alone managing their anxiety effectively.

Enabling versus Taking Accountability

Accountability is one of the most crucial objectives we need to focus on and practice, as well as teach our children and students. When we learn to take accountability for our actions, we are actually taking a significant step toward lowering our anxiety and increasing our overall sense of control.

What Does It Mean to Take Accountability?

Taking accountability means that we are taking complete ownership of our behaviors, choices, and roles. I am specifically referring to taking accountability under stressful circumstances. When we take accountability, we are not blaming others for our choices or behaviors. We are not justifying our actions or making excuses for ourselves. We recognize that we are independently responsible for our actions and the role we played in situations that caused ourselves or others harm or discomfort or resulted in putting ourselves or others at some kind of risk.

When we take ownership of our choices and behaviors, we are better able to recognize how our decisions and actions affect other people. We are more likely to reflect on how we would respond to a situation if someone else made the decision we made. We are better able to consider others' perspectives and understand how others want to be treated.

When we are in a situation that requires us to take accountability for our actions—for example, when we make a mistake at work, forget to do something, or have to cancel on someone—our anxiety is naturally going to go higher on the scale, and our sense of control will drop. If we don't feel like a situation played out the way that it was supposed to, when we recognize that we made a mistake or canceled plans on someone and put them in a difficult situation, we are likely to feel some type of anxiety. We don't feel we have the level of control that we need or want when situations don't turn out the way we planned. In order to bring our anxiety back down on the scale and our sense of control up, we need to take accountability for our actions. We need to recognize that our actions and choices can have a negative outcome, whether it affects us personally or affects others in a negative way. Unfortunately, we can't undo what we have already done. However, we want to manage the situation as best we can by taking accountability for our actions or choices. We need to recognize that we made the choice; no one else made that choice for us.

As we are able to take full ownership of our choices or mistakes, our anxiety will immediately start to decrease, which automatically starts to increase our sense of control. We are doing exactly what we should if we happen to make a mistake or make the wrong choice. We are bound to make mistakes and wrong choices from time to time. After all, we are human. But we want to shift our focus from the fact that we made a mistake to how we handle the situation moving forward. If we make a mistake at work, what would our supervisor want to see? Do you think they want to hear excuses? Do they want to hear us justify our actions? What if we blame others for our actions? They don't want to hear it. All they want is to hear us take accountability for our actions. They will be more accepting of our mistakes if we take ownership of them. They don't want to hear excuses from their employees. They want to know how we are going to handle the situation moving forward. This is the message we want our kids to learn—that it's OK if we make mistakes; the important thing is how we manage our mistakes moving forward, which includes telling the truth. If we teach our kids early how to take accountability, we are setting them up to manage their anxiety more successfully throughout their lives and to gain maturity and the respect of others.

When we start to make excuses, justify, or blame others for our decisions and actions, we are not taking accountability for our behaviors. Doing any of these will cause our anxiety to come down on the scale in that moment, giving us a false sense of control. However, that relief of anxiety is only temporary. Our anxiety will quickly return to a higher level on the scale when we don't take accountability for our actions. In that moment, we are convincing ourselves that what we did was OK and justified, but our actual level of control stays low because we are not taking the proper steps to appropriately manage the situation.

When we *do* take accountability, again, our sense of control will increase because we aren't trying to hide what we did, justify, make excuses, or blame anyone else for our actions or choices. We are likely to understand what we did, that it was our own independent choice, what we need to do differently, and how to manage the situation moving forward. As we take accountability for our actions, there is likely to be a slight increase in anxiety prior to acknowledging our mistake. However, that anxiety will quickly come down once we admit what we've done. If we know what we need to pay attention to moving forward or what we need to do differently, we are increasing our level of control, therefore decreasing our anxiety.

If we think about being in a situation where someone else makes a mistake, how do we feel if they give us an excuse or justify why they did what they did? How do we feel if they blame someone else (or us) for their actions or decisions? What happens to our anxiety level on the scale? It's likely to increase. For myself, I would feel very frustrated if someone was making excuses for their behavior and not taking accountability or acknowledging that what they did was not a good choice. However, if that person took responsibility for their actions and acknowledged how their choice affected others, my frustration/anxiety would go down on the scale. I would feel an increased sense of control because I wouldn't feel I had to convince that person that what they did was wrong. If I felt they understood what they did and were not making excuses, fully accepting that the choice was theirs and understanding what they needed to do moving forward, I would feel like the situation was managed appropriately and there was nothing more I needed to do. Not only would the person who made the mistake bring their own anxiety down and increase their own level of control by taking accountability, but anyone else involved in the situation would also feel their anxiety decrease and sense of control increase.

Another example of when we are able to get control back over our anxiety in a vulnerable situation is when we are pulled over by a police officer while driving. When we see the flashing lights behind us, our anxiety immediately starts to go up. We become nervous, and our thoughts automatically start firing, assuming one thing after another, and very quickly we are anticipating the worst-case scenario. This is another example of how quickly and easily our automatic thoughts trigger our anxiety and take complete control over our mind. We have a very difficult time focusing on what is happening in the moment. Instead, our anxiety takes over, and we struggle to think clearly, even though we have no evidence that our assumptions are absolutely true or definitely going to happen.

Because we struggle to focus in those moments, we automatically go into defense mode when questioned about why we were driving too fast. Oftentimes, that defense mechanism is presented in the form of justification, giving an excuse as to why we were driving so fast or placing blame on others, such as, "Well, the person in front of me was driving the same speed. I was just following him. Why was I the one to get pulled over? Why wasn't the other guy pulled over?"

When we become defensive, our anxiety not only affects us, but it also affects those with whom we are interacting. If a police officer questions us about why we were speeding and all they hear in response are excuses and justification for our actions, they are likely going to react to those defenses by getting annoyed, frustrated, or angry because we are not taking accountability for our actions. When we are making excuses for our behavior, our anxiety might come down slightly on the scale, just for a moment, because in that moment, we are convincing ourselves that what we did was OK. If we can convince ourselves that what we did was OK, then we will feel better. This is a false sense of control. Our anxiety is going to quickly return to a higher level on the scale as we are not exercising appropriate control.

In order to actually bring our level of control up, we need to take accountability for our actions. We need to take ownership of the fact that what we chose to do was not right. When we take accountability for our actions, our anxiety will start to decrease, even if we are not sure of the outcome. However, if we choose not to take accountability for our actions, we can easily get into a power struggle with the police officer, and they will likely continue to move forward with giving us a ticket and making sure that we are held accountable for our actions. If we don't hold ourselves accountable for our actions, someone else will!

Accountability and Addiction

Another example of taking accountability is when someone who has been battling addiction acknowledges that they don't have control over their addictive behavior. There is a reason the first step in battling addiction is to admit that there is a problem. That's because when we admit that we have a problem, we are taking accountability. Without accountability, we are limiting ourselves in being able to do the work that needs to be done to get control over the addiction. Although acknowledging there is a problem with addiction is a first step in its treatment, it typically takes a while for someone to fully understand the breadth of accountability. There is a lot of work involved before someone with an addiction is able to take accountability in all aspects of their life. When someone battling addiction gets to the point where they can fully accept ownership of their actions and choices across all aspects of their life, that is where they make the shift from sobriety to working their recovery. We need to constantly hold ourselves accountable for our behaviors and choices.

This is not only regarding our addictive behaviors but for any behavior or choice in any life domain. If we're only choosing to take accountability sometimes, we're not being honest with ourselves, and we're likely to relapse into maladaptive behavior. We then have to recognize that that was *our* choice, no one else's. We can't justify our actions and still increase our sense of control over the situation. We must take 100 percent accountability for our choices. Once someone battling addiction is able to take accountability for their choices and own their addiction, they will actually increase their awareness and level of control over their addiction. They know that they are now taking the right steps to get control over their addiction. Again, they can't undo what's been done, but they can shift their focus to what they can do moving forward.

Working with an addiction can be tricky when learning to take accountability. Manipulation is often a survival mechanism for someone with an addiction. I use the word *survival* because someone with an addiction will use whatever means necessary to get what they want or need. The addiction fine-tunes an individual to manipulate others or situations in order to get what they think they need. It is difficult to train the brain to think otherwise, to take accountability for their behaviors, when their brain has been programmed to this survival mode to get their substance of choice and prevent them from getting sick.

How Defenses Interfere with Accountability

One reason we often struggle to take accountability is because we don't want to admit when we are wrong, when we make a mistake, when we make a bad decision, or when we flat-out don't have control over something. Unfortunately, we oftentimes interpret these actions as weak and don't want to admit that we are vulnerable. People often assume that something is wrong with us when we are vulnerable. This is a huge misunderstanding. When we take ownership of our actions, we are acknowledging our vulnerability. This is a significant strength. Not only do others have respect for us when we take accountability, but we are increasing our sense of control by addressing our mistakes and vulnerabilities. We are not hiding what we've done but are able to shift our focus to what we can do to manage the situation as best we can. We want to focus on the fact that we are doing the right thing by taking accountability and stay focused on our own responsibilities moving forward.

Respect

There is also the matter of the respect that is given to a person who demonstrates accountability. When a person takes responsibility for their actions, others are likely to respect them for it. Continuing with the example of getting pulled over by a police officer, there is a good chance the officer is going to respect you for taking ownership of your driving behaviors. They are also going to feel less frustrated or anxious if they don't feel they are in a power struggle with you. The officer will be more willing to work with you and may even let you off with a warning rather than handing out a ticket if they see that you understand what you did wrong, accept responsibility, and don't fight it.

Another example is if your supervisor recognizes a mistake you made at work. When they address the issue with you, your anxiety is likely to increase in that moment. You may start to *assume* that your supervisor is going to reprimand you or even that you might lose your job. However, there is no concrete evidence that either of those assumptions is *definitely* going to happen. Your supervisor would like to see how you handle this situation. Are you willing to acknowledge and take accountability for the mistake, or are you going to justify or give an excuse as to why you did what you did? If you choose to take accountability for your actions, your supervisor is more likely to respect how you handled the situation and not feel the need to continue addressing what you did wrong. They will be pleased with the fact that you did not give them any excuses, blame anyone else, or justify your actions. Their level of concern will decrease, and they will feel a greater sense of control when handling the situation. They may initially have felt uncomfortable bringing up a delicate situation with you or correcting you and likely do not want to make you feel bad. If you address the situation appropriately, they are likely to feel more comfortable discussing difficult issues in the future, knowing that you are capable of listening to them, communicating effectively, and taking accountability when needed. In addition, you will feel your anxiety decrease, knowing that you made the right choice by taking accountability.

When working with someone who battles addiction, those who are involved in that person's life will also feel great respect when their loved one has worked their way into recovery after learning to fully take ownership of all the choices they made during their active addiction. They will also see how their loved one continues to take accountability for their choices and actions in the future. This refers to all aspects of life including relationships, work, self-care, daily responsibilities, et cetera.

To summarize what happens to our anxiety when we do and do not take accountability for our actions:

- We might alleviate our anxiety in the moment when we are justifying our behaviors or manipulating others; however, this is only a false sense of control. Our anxiety will drop briefly on the scale but will quickly return to a higher level if we are not acknowledging our role in that situation. We need to be honest with ourselves as well as others if we expect to gain adequate control and bring our anxiety down. By taking accountability for our actions, we know we are doing the right thing, we are not making excuses or justifying our behaviors, we are being honest, and we are not manipulating the situation to our benefit. We are simply acknowledging our role or the choice that we made. This allows us to shift our focus to what we need to do moving forward to improve the situation or prevent it from happening again. Furthermore, when we take accountability for our actions, others are more likely to respect us for taking ownership of making a mistake.

- Others will be less likely to feel anxiety toward us (frustration, annoyance, or anger) for making a mistake if we are able to take full responsibility. When we don't take responsibility for our actions, others often feel frustration toward us, which makes the dynamic more volatile, possibly leading to a power struggle. Person A might point out what person B did, person B becomes defensive and justifies their behavior/choice, leading to person A becoming more frustrated and defensive while continuing to express what person B did that was wrong, while person B is now reactive and talking over person A, so person A raises their voice, and each person is fighting to have control or the upper hand in the situation. Neither person feels like they are being heard. Person B might be feeling attacked, which makes it difficult for them to take accountability for their actions, all this resulting in a power struggle where neither person feels they have control or have been heard or respected.

Enabling

When we (and kids) are not taught how to take accountability for our actions or understand the importance of it, we struggle to accept when things don't go our way or when we don't get what we want. Kids are going to engage in various behaviors when they don't get what they want upon initial request (or demand!). As kids are learning how to navigate their environment, they become master manipulators. This is actually their job when they are toddlers and in latency (between six and twelve years of age). They are trying to figure out what they can get away with and what they can't. This is why it is critical for us as adults to make sure that we are teaching our kids accountability, how to accept when they don't get their way, the importance of the word *no*, and ways they can communicate in order to get their needs met more effectively while exercising control in appropriate and healthy ways.

When our kids ask us for something and our response to them is no, they will likely escalate the situation (especially when they are younger) and start to plead or beg for what they want. When the answer is still no, they might continue to up the ante and whine, present a negative attitude, cry, or have a meltdown. Although it is often hard to manage these behaviors, we need to be aware that we are not to enable our kids. If our kids keep up these behaviors and we ultimately give them what they want because we just can't stand listening to the whining or meltdowns, we are giving them what they want. They just learned that if they keep increasing their behaviors, they can manipulate us (or, in their minds, trick us) into giving them what they want. The next time they want something and don't get it right away, they know they can eventually break us and get what they want. By giving them what they want, we are enabling them. We aren't teaching them that they have to accept no as an answer sometimes. They aren't learning that they don't always get their way or that things don't always go as planned. We aren't teaching them how to accept that they don't have control over everything or everyone. We aren't teaching them to identify what else they can do in the moment or to find another time when they might be able to do what they want. We are not teaching them how to problem-solve on their own. We are enabling them. This is why it is so critical for parents and caregivers to be consistent in setting limits and following through with them.

Let's think about what enabling looks like for someone battling addiction (young adult or older), living at home with their parents. When parents first learn about their child's addiction, their instinct is to help their child in any way they can, which is understandable. Any parent would hate to see their child struggling with an addiction. It's natural to automatically think about how you can help your child and want to do whatever it takes. However, this is a slippery slope. The child who has the addiction is responsible for themselves and their own treatment. Parents might be able to financially support their child's treatment, but if the child does not take accountability in doing the work to get control over their addiction, they end up being enabled if they know that their parents will continue to pay for their treatment and still provide them with a place to live, food, and financial support, particularly if the child continues to use. Although it is very difficult, it is important for parents to be firm and consistent in setting limits with their child and holding them accountable for their addiction and other harmful or risky choices. Parents can still support their child through communication, listening, and asking questions about what they are doing to take care of themselves, but it's critical to set firm boundaries between the parents and child.

Resilience

Resilience is a very important aspect of overcoming anxiety and life-altering events, traumatic or otherwise. According to the American Psychological Association (APA), resilience is the process of adapting well in the face of adversity, trauma, tragedy, threats, or significant sources of stress and overcoming difficult life experiences. In other words, using Control Theory, resilience is identifying ways in which we can exercise or gain back control in areas of our lives that have been altered or traumatized. This involves processing various emotions, understanding the thought process behind the traumatic experience, and understanding where we feel a loss of control.

The APA lists a few factors that are associated with resilience; however, it does not address the neuropsychological aspect of mental health when it comes to resilience. One important factor is the ability to make realistic plans. This is consistent with the idea in Control Theory of identifying what is within our control and focusing on what we can do to help manage the stressful situation moving forward. This is where we focus on solutions. By identifying possible options to help in a stressful or potentially stressful situation, we are already focusing on what is within our control. Therefore, our sense of control starts to immediately increase. Again, when our sense of control increases, our anxiety simultaneously decreases.

By identifying more than one option to manage a stressor, we are utilizing flexibility in thinking, as well as building on new adaptive neural networks, versus staying stuck in a neural network of what doesn't go well or the way we want. As previously discussed, flexibility in thinking allows us to modify our plans or options according to the situation. When we think too rigidly, we are vulnerable to experiencing higher levels of stress when our only plan does not go as intended. We can be easily caught off guard and not know what to do if things don't go according to plan when we have such rigid thinking. It is very difficult to think about other possibilities. Flexibility in thinking also helps us accept things over which we don't have control and allows us to shift our focus to what we can do given the circumstances in which we find ourselves, helping us identify what is actually within our control.

This taps into another point that neuropsychologists address in understanding the physiology of the brain when experiencing chronic stress. The hippocampus aids in bringing perspective when assessing stressful situations. As previously mentioned, the hippocampus draws on memories from past experiences and information that we already learned and puts our current stressful situation into context, helping facilitate our problem-solving abilities. We can then draw on what possible solutions might work in a given situation and what we know hasn't worked before. We can deduct from previous experiences or what we've learned from others, apply that information to our current situation, and identify possible options to help manage our current stressor.

Stress hormones can help us remember important information so that we are able to recall dangerous situations to avoid them in the future. The hormones help provide a natural defense mechanism and help prepare us to better manage the potential stressor if it happens again. The parts of the brain responsible for learning and memory are also the ones with the most stress hormones (Stixrud & Johnson, 2018; Center for Studies on Human Stress, 2017). These are the areas that receive the most information about a stressor. When too many or too few stress hormones are activated, our memory is affected.

High levels of stress interfere with our ability to learn new information and to accurately encode, interpret, or recall information (van der Kolk, 2015; Sweeton, 2019). This is one reason students might draw a blank when taking a test, even though they understand the material. Because students are often juggling many responsibilities and are under high stress, their ability to learn new information or recall learned information can be limited.

As previously mentioned, the amygdala, prefrontal cortex, hippocampus, insula, and cingulate are critical in learning, memory, and anxiety management. The prefrontal cortex evaluates the stressful situation to help us make decisions about what to do. The hippocampus is responsible for spatial memory, helping us identify or recall where we encounter a stressor. The amygdala is responsible for our emotional memory, such as fear or threats. All these areas play critical roles in helping us navigate anxiety-provoking life experiences. By identifying information about the stressor, we are then able to utilize our problem-solving skills to shift our sense of control back into our own hands. However, when we experience chronic stress, which results from repeated exposure to stressors that lead to the release of hormones, it causes wear and tear on the mind and body (Stixrud & Johnson, 2018). We have a more difficult time recovering from repeated exposure to stressors and processing important information or memories to help us manage the stressors as effectively as we should.

As Dr. Stixrud addresses, acute or short-term stress is an important factor in resilience. Acute stress, according to Dr. Stixrud, occurs during events or situations that include novelty, unpredictability, or a threat to our sense of self and leave us with a poor sense of control. Short-term or intermittent anxiety allows us to recover from the high level of anxiety we experience during that event and use it in a productive way. Acute stress can be helpful because we are able to learn from these experiences more quickly, and the hormones that are released help us manage the situation. This is different from chronic, ongoing anxiety, from which it is more difficult to recover.

Other important factors associated with resilience, according to the APA, are communication and problem-solving. This is also consistent with Control Theory as we emphasize the importance of communication. As previously discussed, communication is one of the biggest tools in exercising control in a healthy and effective way. It's a way in which we can express our emotions, process our thoughts (vocalize any assumptions or anticipatory thoughts and have others clarify information that may have led to those thoughts), set boundaries with others (where we are essentially letting others know that we are in control of ourselves, not anyone else, and don't allow others to manipulate or project their own anxiety onto us), and hold others accountable for their own responsibilities rather than allowing others to place their responsibilities on us.

Problem-solving is key to Control Theory and stems from Cognitive Theory. In Control Theory, we work to focus on what is within our control at the present moment and identify what our options are moving forward. Solution-focused therapy is one treatment objective that we use with Control Theory to identify specific steps in helping manage a stressful situation or circumstance. The objective is to help an overwhelming, high-anxiety situation become more manageable. By identifying options that are at our disposal or within our control to manage a potentially stressful situation as best we can, we are automatically increasing our sense of control. This, again, requires flexibility in thinking.

By exercising flexibility in thinking and focusing on other options that are within our control, while accepting what is *not* within our control, we are preventing ourselves from thinking rigidly. If our plan does not go the way we predicted, we don't feel we lose complete control because we have other options. This is what the solution-focused treatment objectives address. By coming up with a plan of how to manage a potentially stressful situation, we are going to feel more prepared if the situation actually materializes. We will have already thought through our options and identified what is within our control. We are more prepared. This preparation in and of itself increases our sense of control immediately, which also decreases our anxiety. Once we identify a plan, we put that plan aside and then focus on what we need to do in the moment. Again, we don't have proof that what we're anticipating will definitely happen, and if it's not currently happening, we want to put our plan aside and shift our focus to what we need to do in the moment. We need a strong cingulate in order to keep bringing our focus back to what we need to do in the moment.

Self-confidence is another factor the APA lists as being associated with resilience. This is also consistent with Control Theory when applying a scale from zero to ten, where self-confidence goes hand in hand with our sense of control. As previously discussed, if we feel competent in certain areas of our lives or know that we have certain strengths and skills, we are going to feel a greater sense of control. Thus, when we feel we have more control, we are more confident that we will be equipped to manage stressors that arise in the future. If we know what we're capable of doing, we can better predict what we can do to manage a stressful situation. However, in order to strengthen our self-confidence, we need to understand and consistently pay attention to how we are feeling physically, as well as mentally, in order to properly manage our anxiety.

Neurologically, if we practice specific bottom-up and top-down (cognitive) exercises to help reregulate the amygdala, strengthen the PFC, strengthen the hippocampus, reregulate the insula, and strengthen the cingulate, we are also increasing neurogenesis (Sweeton, 2019). This means that we are able to grow new neurons and build new networks to help overcome the damage done by anxiety and trauma. We can undo the damage done by the cortisol on the hippocampus, causing issues with memory. We can literally strengthen and repair damaged structures of the brain, helping us to become more resilient to future anxiety.

Taking Care of Ourselves

Self-care is critical in helping manage anxiety. As we just left off with resilience, we are able to grow new neurons (particularly in the hippocampus) to help repair structures in the brain, known as neurogenesis. Unfortunately, neurogenesis decreases with age, which is why it is so important for us to take steps that are within our control to help take care of our health as best we can. The two other most significant factors that prevent neurogenesis is marijuana use and experiencing chronic anxiety (Sweeton, 2019). There are some things we can do to help increase neurogenesis, such as exercise, novelty (doing something new), dance, yoga, and incorporating omega 3s into our diet.

There are some other important factors that play a direct role in how anxious we might feel on a daily basis. One of the main factors that highly influence our anxiety is sleep. As previously discussed, when we don't get the amount of sleep that we need or the quality of sleep that we need, we are automatically more vulnerable to developing higher levels of anxiety. We have a harder time focusing or concentrating; we are more irritable, have less patience, and are more likely to react quickly and negatively in stressful situations.

Some of the basic self-care objectives that we are able to have greater control over in addition to exercise and eating healthy include making sure that we eat something for breakfast to help improve our cognitive functioning, creating a consistent sleep-wake routine, limiting our intake of caffeine, alcohol, and alternate substances. Exercising does not need to be extreme—even a ten-minute walk every day, for example, can help.

I recommend limiting caffeine intake, especially in the afternoon. I typically recommend not having any caffeine after 12:00 p.m. as the caffeine stays in our system for up to twelve hours. If we have a cup of coffee at 4:00 p.m., the caffeine will still be at half its strength six hours later when we are trying to fall asleep, therefore interfering with our getting the deep, restful sleep we need.

Eating breakfast is also critical in helping us manage our anxiety more effectively. When we don't get the nutrients we need, especially after several hours of fasting overnight, we have a harder time focusing, concentrating, and managing stressors as effectively as we should. These are things that we can choose to implement into our daily routines that help facilitate our ability to perform better across domains as well as helping us manage our anxiety more effectively.

Understanding Relapse

What does it mean to relapse? Relapsing is reengaging in maladaptive behavior, usually in a time of high stress. Relapse can happen after we started working on abstaining from engaging in our maladaptive behaviors for any period of time.

We are all vulnerable to relapse when we are experiencing a high level of anxiety. Relapse can happen when we are having a difficult time identifying our automatic thoughts or the source of the anxiety and have been struggling to focus on ourselves and what our responsibilities are in the moment. We are particularly vulnerable to relapse when we struggle to take accountability for our actions and choices. It is critical to understand the importance of this responsibility we have to ourselves.

Let's recall what can easily happen when our anxiety is at the top of the scale, and we are feeling entirely overwhelmed. When we are completely consumed by our anxiety, the easiest thing for us to do in the moment is engage in whatever is at our fingertips, whether it be blaming others, substance use, self-harm, or any other type of avoidance. Avoidance is the easiest defense mechanism to help alleviate our anxiety. Unfortunately, it is much easier to engage in the old maladaptive behaviors we are so used to or conditioned to. It takes more work, mentally, emotionally, and cognitively, to take the appropriate steps to decrease our anxiety in a healthy way. It takes work to resist the impulses that can bring us temporary relief so quickly, often immediately.

When we are experiencing such a high level of anxiety that it is consuming us, we are not able to think clearly or focus on what we are in control of in the moment. This is why it is critical for us to learn how to use cognitive objectives as a preventative measure, so we don't continue to engage in the maladaptive behaviors we are so used to in a time of high stress or crisis. It takes constant practice to become more aware of anxiety, understand how we perceive and interpret information, be able to identify our automatic thoughts, recognize what thoughts are valid or not, identify what our options are when experiencing high anxiety (problem-solve), shift our focus to what we are doing in the moment, and identify what is within our control. It takes continuous practice to shift our focus from what others are doing around us or trying to meet others' expectations to what we need to be doing for ourselves and what is in our own best interests. We are essentially reconditioning our brain to think differently than it's been doing our entire lives. This takes time. However, as we practice these objectives, we will be decreasing the likelihood of a relapse as well as the duration, intensity, and frequency of symptoms caused by anxiety, including depression. By increasing our level of control over our anxiety, we will be increasing our level of control across all areas of our lives.

Medication

Medication can be a controversial subject. It has been very rare for me to recommend my clients for medication in addition to therapy when specifically practicing CBT. The reason I seldom recommend my clients for medication is that I feel CBT, Control Theory, and providing education on the psychoneurobiology of the brain are very successful based on the amount of progress I see in my clients within a short period of time. I tend to see progress with my clients very early in their treatment if they choose to apply the clinical work they are learning in therapy in their daily lives. The more effort and practice my clients put into managing their anxiety, the more progress I see, and the faster I see it.

If I see progress with a client, I interpret that as the client better understanding their anxiety and starting to practice skills that allow them to increase their self-reliance rather than depending on someone or something else to help them feel better. When they start to see evidence that they have the power to decrease their anxiety because of the steps they are taking, not only does their overall sense of control increase and their baseline average daily level of anxiety decrease, but their self-confidence and happiness increase as well.

Although it's rare that I recommend that my clients take medication, I am not completely opposed to using it. When I have been working with a client for a few sessions and have some time to assess their anxiety and how they have been managing it over a few weeks' time, I am able to gather enough information to see how intense their anxiety is on a day-to-day and week- to-week-basis. I will also be able to assess if my client is willing or even able to do the clinical work if their anxiety is extremely high. Medication is to be used to help the client's anxiety decrease a couple of notches on the scale to the point where they can focus a little more clearly, have better concentration, and are able to think through the clinical steps that are needed to decrease their anxiety. When the nervous system is on overdrive, where a person's Stress Response System is continuously activated and they can't easily recover from their anxiety, they can't do any cognitive work when in this state. They may need medication to help slightly decrease the activation of the SRS. Medication can be particularly helpful if someone is battling chronic anxiety, depression, or past or present trauma. We need to tap into the amygdala to calm it down and get the frontal lobe back online for us to be able to do any cognitive work. Medication is not supposed to take anxiety or depression away. It is not supposed to numb the client. It is supposed to help alleviate the anxiety to the point where they are then able to do the clinical work to bring their anxiety down to a more manageable level on a day-to-day basis.

Unfortunately, it is very rare that I have a client who has either been on medication or goes on medication who is taught how to use their medication appropriately by the prescribing doctor. Medication for anxiety (or depression or any other mental health symptoms) should be used in conjunction with therapy. When clients are not utilizing therapy while taking medication to manage mental health symptoms, they are not increasing their level of awareness of their anxiety. They are becoming more dependent on the medication to help them feel better, often expecting the medication to take all their symptoms away and are not understanding why they are feeling anxious (or depressed) in the first place. They are not learning where their anxiety originates or how their thought patterns are triggering their anxiety. They are not becoming educated about their anxiety and, therefore, are not increasing their skills to manage their anxiety or depression. They are dependent on a foreign substance to manage their symptoms.

Let's review what we discussed about defense mechanisms and substance use. If we are high on the scale and don't have the awareness or the clinical tools to help manage and appropriately control our anxiety, we often use whatever is at our fingertips to help alleviate that awful feeling of being at an 8, 9, or 10 on the scale. There are numerous behaviors in which we can engage to help alleviate that terror as we've previously discussed. These maladaptive behaviors can help us feel better in the moment, so we don't have to do the work to reflect on what our responsibility is to ourselves or what the steps are to manage our anxiety or depression appropriately and healthily.

However, these options will only bring temporary relief. Our anxiety is going to go right back up on the scale. These behaviors will give us a false sense of control. Medication will serve the same purpose of helping us feel better. However, medication does not take away the source of anxiety and doesn't teach us how to manage the anxiety ourselves when not used in conjunction with therapy. Medication, when used alone, overprescribed, or not used the right way, impairs our ability to feel pleasure or curiosity, to grow and develop emotionally and intellectually, and to become contributing members of society. Medications are often prescribed instead of teaching people the skills to manage their distressing physical sensations (van der Kolk, 2015).

Therefore, I believe it is highly important to educate my clients on how the brain works under the weight of anxiety and trauma. When I'm able to present more concrete information as to how anxiety affects our functioning and provide ways in which we can exercise specific structures of the brain to overcome anxiety and trauma, we will be able to not only change the neurobiology of our brains but maintain these changes and live a more functional life on a day-to-day basis. We become more reliant on the cognitive and neurological work that we do, versus becoming dependent on medication or a foreign substance that won't have any healthy or long-lasting effect on anxiety management. Just like any other substance, we can eventually become dependent on the medication to help us feel better rather than depending on our problem-solving skills to get control over the anxiety.

Over time, we build up a tolerance to the medication. As a result, the dose of the medication is increased, or another medication is added to the prescription to help manage the symptoms. Ultimately, many people end up having their medications continuously increased, whether by the dose or by adding supplemental medications or having to go through medication changes. This can cause side effects, which can be detrimental or create additional stressors to our daily functioning. When is this pattern going to end if we aren't taught how to actively manage our anxiety? Who wants to be dependent on medication for the rest of their lives for something that can be healthily and naturally controlled? Let's at least minimize the amount of medication we are on if necessary and work on building up our own sense of control and self-confidence in being able to tackle anxiety and know that we are capable of taking care of ourselves.

Again, if there is any progress in our clinical work (becoming more aware of how our body feels under anxiety and being able to work with our body to settle our nervous system, being aware of our baseline level of anxiety, understanding our thought patterns and how we interpret information or situations, or identifying what we are able to do to manage a stressful situation as best we can), resulting in even a slight decrease in anxiety, then there is evidence that we are depending on our own skills to help manage our anxiety. Let's not assume that medication is a necessity from the start.

Screen Time

Another factor that affects our cognitive functioning is screen time. It's important to understand the extent to which screen time can impair the developing brain. Studies on screen time have consistently found that it has negative effects on the cognitive development of children, particularly those under the age of three. A study done by the US Department of Health and Human Services found that, on average, American children spend seven hours a day on electronic devices. (This includes television, iPads, iPods, smartphones, computers, and video games.) According to Dr. Aric Sigman at the British Psychological Society, screen time impedes a child's brain in developing specific abilities, such as focus, concentration, recognizing other people's tone of voice and emotions, communication, and even building their vocabularies. This damage can potentially be permanent. Children under the age of three are in what is considered the "critical period" of the developing brain. The way in which a child's brain develops during the critical period affects how the brain continues to develop and function throughout the child's life (Margalit, 2016). In other words, the critical period lays the foundation on which the child's brain continues to develop. Children need to be exposed to specific natural stimuli in order for their brains to develop healthily, specifically during the critical period. These natural stimuli need to come from the outside environment.

The stimuli that children need are not provided by electronic devices. By not getting the natural stimulation they need for their brains to grow, their development becomes stunted (Margalit, 2016). Children need to learn how to process emotions and communicate with others, understand how others communicate with them, learn what different tones of voice mean, and even be able to visualize pictures and follow a storyline. When kids spend too much time on a screen, they are not using their own cognitive skills to figure things out. The device does the work for them, and they become lazy.

The frontal lobe, which is responsible for interpreting and comprehending social interactions, including facial expressions, and discerning tone of voice, is developed through "authentic human interaction" (Margalit, 2016). The frontal lobe's most critical time of development is in early childhood. When kids have limited personal interactions because they spend excessive amounts of time in front of a screen, their emotional development and ability to read social cues can be stunted, potentially indefinitely.

Another important point that Margalit (2016) addresses is that when babies and children spend a significant amount of time in front of a screen, especially when they are using an interactive device, such as an iPad, smartphone, or video game, they become conditioned to receiving immediate gratification. Just as when adults engage in an activity that brings pleasure, as kids are able to swipe a screen to bring about new colors, images, and other stimuli, the neurotransmitter dopamine is released in the brain. Dopamine brings a feeling of pleasure and is a rewarding response. When children become used to this feeling of immediate gratification, they prefer this type of rewarding feeling to engaging in real interpersonal interactions. This behavior response is tantamount to behaviors in which adults engage, such as substance use, self-harm, and other risky behaviors, which help bring a temporary sense of relief or pleasure. In Control Theory, using electronic devices brings a false sense of control to children when they are conditioned to getting a desired response immediately and feeling an immediate sense of reward and pleasure.

According to Dr. Stixrud, every hour of screen time for a child is associated with increased blood pressure, while every hour of reading is associated with decreased blood pressure. He also states that the more technology kids use, the poorer their self-regulation is, and their executive functioning worsens. Self-regulation and executive functioning are twice as good at predicting academic performance success as IQ at all grade levels.

Anxiety and Its Relationship to Sleep

Sleep is one of the most critical factors, if not *the* most critical factor, in influencing anxiety. Sleep can directly affect a person's level of anxiety. According to Dr. Michael Breus and the National Sleep Foundation (Breus, 2017), adolescents require between eight and ten hours of sleep per night, while adults require between seven and eight, and younger children need between ten and thirteen. When we don't get the amount of sleep we need, or a high quality of sleep, we are more vulnerable to experiencing higher levels of anxiety. According to Dr. Breus, research has found that only approximately 15 percent of adolescents are getting sufficient sleep. It is highly critical that adolescents receive consistent, quality sleep because their brains are still developing. They are highly vulnerable to experiencing health and safety issues and struggling with performance, focus, attention, ability to learn, information retention, and their overall cognitive functioning when they are not getting their required sleep.

Sleep cycles for adolescents differ from those of adults and young children. Adolescents' hormones, particularly the hormone melatonin, shift to a later sleep-wake schedule and are triggered later in the evening than those of adults and younger children (Breus, 2017). As a result, adolescents tend to naturally get tired and go to sleep later at night, closer to eleven o'clock p.m., while adults are more likely to fall asleep earlier. Therefore, adolescents tend to want to sleep later in the morning than adults. According to Breus, melatonin starts to work in the late afternoon for most adults; however, it has a delayed cycle with adolescents, and therefore the melatonin level drops off earlier in the morning in adults than in adolescents.

The brain is very active, even when we are sleeping. Sleep is when our body physically repairs itself, cleans out waste materials that can be harmful to our health, and processes and condenses emotional information (Breus, 2017). Sleep is critical for the still-developing adolescent brain. The brain's prefrontal cortex is not fully developed and is the last part of the brain to reach full development. This is the part of the brain that is responsible for emotional regulation, decision making, and other executive functioning. Breus further supports that sleep deprivation in adolescents can lead to cognitive impairments, including:

- trouble with memory
- diminished focus and concentration
- impaired learning
- difficulty making healthy and safe choices
- increased risk of engaging in risky behaviors as well as aggressive and impulsive behaviors and choices
- poor judgment and decision making (and other psychosocial stressors)
- emotional issues, including:
  - struggling with emotional regulation
  - irritability
  - increased generalized anxiety
  - greater risk for depression and suicidal thoughts, social withdrawal, aggressiveness, and difficulty getting along with others
- struggles with academic performance (including increased absences or tardiness)

To highlight how important sleep is for our health, let's look at some research. A study conducted using lab rats found that rats died as quickly if they were prevented from sleeping as they did if prevented from eating (Lambert, 2005). Other research found that sleep deprivation produces similar effects on the mind and body as chronic stress (McEwen & Karatsoreos, 2015). This research also found increases in cortisol levels, reaction to stress, and blood pressure and decreased efficacy in the functioning of the parasympathetic nervous system, which is supposed to calm us. Sleep deprivation also produces inflammation, affects insulin production, decreases appetite, and depresses mood. This finding is consistent with Control Theory, in which a lack of sleep increases anxiety, therefore decreasing our sense of control, focus, concentration, and self-regulation and increasing irritability.

There is no difference in performance on cognitive tests between older adolescents who sleep four to six hours per night for six weeks and those who don't get any sleep for three days. This study suggests that six hours of sleep or less is equivalent to chronic sleep deficiency. With sleep deficiency, the amygdala becomes more reactive in response to emotionally charged events, mimicking brain activity when experiencing high anxiety. This research is consistent with the neuropsychological theory of anxiety and control by Dr. Stixrud. These findings are also consistent with Control Theory. When we misinterpret information and make assumptions, we react more impulsively, decreasing our ability to think logically. We become more reactive than responsive. According to this study, our ability to see things in proper context is impaired, which then impairs our judgment.

Based on this information alone, it is evident how critical it is for children and adolescents to get the recommended (really required) amount of sleep. Students need to prioritize their sleep over staying up past what should be their natural bedtime doing their academic work. When students continuously sacrifice their sleep in an effort to complete their schoolwork, they are putting themselves at greater risk for more significant issues, as well as impeding proper brain development. These are both short- and long-term consequences, but this lack of sleep can ultimately have lifelong effects on physical, emotional, and mental health.

It is critical that schools, teachers, and the entire educational system take their students' sleep into account. The priority should not be on the amount of work placed on students. The priority needs to be on the health of the students. Without support for their needs and efforts to take care of their health, mental health, and sleep in particular, students will not be able to perform at an optimal level academically, physically, or even socially. If we are expecting our students to perform at their highest level at all times (which is an unrealistic expectation in and of itself), then we need to support their need for sleep and self-care. Furthermore, if students don't learn how to self-regulate (be aware of and monitor what their bodies and minds need), care for themselves, and manage their time effectively when they are adolescents, then we are setting them up for a lifelong struggle of anxiety and stress.

Continuing on the trajectory of minimal sleep and research findings, research from various sources has found a strong correlation between insufficient sleep and depression. Unfortunately, adolescents are more likely to use caffeine, nicotine, alcohol, or drugs to help manage their mood swings than to get sufficient sleep or learn appropriate ways to effectively manage their anxiety when they are tired. According to Control Theory, the less sleep we get, the more vulnerable we are to higher levels of anxiety, and the longer we are in a cycle of restricted sleep and increased anxiety. Eventually, we hit a wall and feel we can't keep battling anxiety anymore. We start to experience symptoms of depression when we hit that wall. Competitive academics are not worth jeopardizing brain development or emotional regulation. It puts young people at a higher risk of developing anxiety and depression while simultaneously diminishing their sense of self-worth. These are long-term, potentially life-altering effects just to finish an assignment that has no bearing on how successful a student will be throughout their life.

Another study that Dr. Stixrud references involved two groups of sixth graders. One group was asked to sleep one hour more than usual for three nights, while the other group was asked to sleep one hour less than usual for three nights. The study found that students who had as little as thirty-five minutes less sleep than the others performed at a fourth-grade level on cognitive tests, effectively losing two years of cognitive ability (Sadeh et al., 2003). According to Dr. Stixrud, numerous studies have found a correlation between weaker academic performance and self-reported decreased sleep time. There are also studies of more than nine thousand students showing decreases in absences and tardiness, more alertness in school, and improved mood (which means a decrease in anxiety!) in schools that have later start times (Wahlstrom, 2002).

So how do you work with your child when they aren't prioritizing their sleep? Here are some guidelines:

- Start by presenting a choice: "You can choose to go to bed at a reasonable time (demonstrating responsibility), and you will be able to perform better in school tomorrow (as well as feel better, feel less anxious, be able to manage stress more effectively, etc.). If you choose not to go to sleep at a reasonable time, you are choosing to make yourself more vulnerable to feeling anxious and not being able to focus, concentrate, or perform at the level you need or want. If your performance and grades are important to you, I hope you choose to make sleep a priority in order to do your best."

- Promote winding down in the evening, creating a routine to help your child fall asleep or get into sleep mode. For example, stop any screen time (phones, television, computer, video games, iPads, etc.) about one hour before bedtime. Have them do a quiet activity (reading, taking a shower, meditation, listening to music, etc.).

- Have them do screen-time homework earlier in the evening.

- Encourage tech-free zones in the house.

- Limit screen time, especially an hour before bedtime.

- Foster a consistent bedtime for every age.

- Have them abstain from any caffeine, which can trigger anxiety itself as well as interfering with their sleep cycle.

- Use light exposure in the morning to help reset their circadian clock and reestablish an appropriate sleep-wake cycle.

Part IV: Control Theory in Practice

Anxiety and Trauma Treatment and Mirror Neurons

The goal with Control Theory is to gain a stronger sense of personal control and self-agency. As Dr. van der Kolk states, our agency starts with what scientists call interoception—our awareness of our sensory and body-based feelings: the greater that awareness, the greater our potential to control our lives. Unfortunately, most people are not in-tune with their bodies, making it difficult to recognize when their bodies are communicating with them. Dr. van der Kolk presents a much more in-depth description of this. According to Dr. van der Kolk, sensorimotor (bottom-up or body-based work) approaches are to:

1.) Draw out the sensory information that is blocked and frozen by trauma.
2.) Help patients befriend (versus suppress) the energies released by that inner experience.
3.) Complete the self-preserving physical actions that were thwarted when they were trapped, restrained, or immobilized by terror.

Applying this to Control Theory, when our personal sense of control is taken away, trauma enters. Self-regulation requires us to be in tune with our bodies and bodily sensations. Anxiety will manifest as symptoms; however, most people will only acknowledge the symptoms and not the precipitating stressor. Panic symptoms are maintained in part due to activation of negative neural networks, which is also strengthened and maintained by a fear of bodily sensations associated with panic attacks. With trauma, the body is always on guard. It is always in a defensive state (van der Kolk, 2015; Sweeton, 2019). It has difficulty relaxing or feeling safe.

The standard medical practice is to focus on treating our symptoms with a specific drug versus trying to find the root cause of the distress or understand how our problems interfere with our ability to function in society (van der Kolk, 2015). As Dr. van der Kolk states, the body remembers trauma. It is a sensory disorder, not a cognitive disorder, resulting in autoimmune disorders, muscular-skeletal disorders, and even cancer (van der Kolk, 2015; Maté, 2021). There needs to be a shift in how we treat trauma and mental health.

Eye Movement Desensitization and Reprocessing (EMDR) treatment specifically targets our neural networks—by identifying key experiences of our past, present, and future anticipations, we tap into and activate the negative neural networks. Remember the rules of neuroplasticity, in order to work with past anxieties or traumas, we need to activate that network first. After activating the network, we then work to desensitize the negative, maladaptive network. Eventually we introduce information, context or evidence that demonstrates we are capable of successfully managing our anxiety and strengthen our personal sense of self and self-control. In a study comparing the use of Prozac to EMDR for patients with Post-Traumatic Stress Disorder and depression, EMDR proved to be a more effective antidepressant than Prozac (van der Kolk, 2015).

The most important factor in any kind of therapy, and the most critical objective that we can provide for our kids in facilitating healthy brain development and repairing any developmental disruptions on the brain is establishing a rapport with our kids, or a therapeutic alliance (van der Kolk, 2015; Sweeton, 2019). Because anxiety and trauma are physical experiences, we need to establish a safe environment and relationship with whom we work in order to have the most positive and successful outcome in treatment. Establishing a therapeutic alliance is also a physical experience, not a cognitive method. It's a bottom-up approach (working through the body to change the brain) to help regulate the nervous system.

The therapeutic alliance counts for more of the outcome variants than any other tool (van der Kolk, 2015; Sweeton, 2019). Forming an alliance is the most evidence-based objective that we can provide. There is no other one technique that explains outcomes better than the relationship (van der Kolk, 2015). The therapeutic alliance provides a reparative experience for those who have experienced trauma (van der Kolk, 2015; Sweeton, 2019). Our brains interact with and influence other brains. There are studies that show that brain waves align when people make eye contact and "attune" (Sweeton, 2019). Mothers can soothe infants and reduce cortisol levels by focusing on them using their PFC through eye contact and touch. The safest way to protect against anxiety and trauma is social support (van der Kolk, 2015).

The mechanism behind the alliance is through mirror neurons. The brain can actually interact with and influence other brains. Brain waves align when people make eye contact and "attune" with one another (Sweeton, 2019). The neuroscience of alliance starts with attachment. Mothers can soothe infants and reduce cortisol levels by focusing on them using their pre-frontal cortex (through eye contact and touch). We are wired to connect to others, to co-regulate with others. Eye contact activates the PFC and decreases amygdala activation and decreases cortisol (van der Kolk, 2015; Sweeton, 2019). The ANS is always shaped and regulated through interactions with others. You want your child to meet your calmness, versus you meeting their chaos. The child then feels safe and contained. In other words, they feel in control. Through this, they learn to regulate emotions, which helps them navigate relationships and have attuned communication, empathy, insight, awareness, and response flexibility (being able to pause, evaluate options, and make appropriate decisions).During these interactions, mirror neurons are activated in the emotional centers of the brain.

There is a link between particular neurons in our brains and others' actions. The brain contains a system of neurons that fire in response to the intentional actions of others, as well as when we perform those same actions. (Gallese, Fadiga, Fogassi, & Rizzolatti, 1996). (Emphasizing the importance in modeling for our kids/students.) The best way to activate mirror neurons is through the right hemisphere, which is engaged in attunement and attachment (Sweeton, 2019). There are mirror neurons in the amygdala (as well as the PFC and insula) that are influenced by our interactions with others. Mirror neurons are what allow students to have a different, reparative experience (hopefully). Students can re-learn and heal attachment.

Mirror neurons in the emotional centers of our brain are what allow us to form empathy and are the basis for the therapeutic alliance (van der Kolk, 2015; Sweeton, 2019). They allow us to merge experiences with others. The therapeutic alliance is what creates change in the brain, helping establish healthier attachments and reparative relationships. However, we still need to be mindful of setting emotional boundaries with others. Can you recall a time (or many times) when you've been feeling fine and then start talking with another person and suddenly felt anxious or uncomfortable? Or felt tension when walking into a room with others? You can feel their anxiety. There is a merging of emotional experiences as brains influence one another. We need to make sure that we set appropriate boundaries with others as our different roles require. We have different boundaries with our parents than we do with our friends, or our teachers, or our therapists. There are ways in which we engage with our friends that would be inappropriate with our therapists. We need to establish healthy boundaries for all of our relationships. Our parents/caretakers are responsible for teaching us and modeling for us appropriate boundaries in our relationships with others. Once again, it is critical for our kids to have healthy, safe attachments with their caregivers. This also connects back to how the amygdala is hyperactive in kids before two years of age, and that they need to experience healthy attachments and safe environments in order to start pruning neurons in the amygdala to calm it down so that it's not as reactive. The mirror neurons are an important component of the attachment process.

To give you some more context as to how mirror neurons work in the different parts of the brain, there are mirror neurons in the sensory and motor strips of our cortex. These areas of the cortex are activated when we watch others in action. However, there is a physical boundary that is constantly communicating to our brain that what I am seeing someone else do is in fact happening to that other person and not myself, even though my motor cortex is activated while watching the other person. That boundary that communicates to my brain that "That is that other person, and this is me", is our skin. Our skin is constantly sending sensory information up to our brain. So, when we see someone fall, we might cringe, but are still well aware of the fact that it happened to another person, and it wasn't us that fell. Or when watching a scary movie, we might jump in our seats or get goose bumps, but we know that what is happening in the movie, is not happening to me. However, when it comes to the emotional centers of our brain, there is no boundary that tells us that the emotional experience we're having is not ours, but in fact it's someone else's anxiety that we're experiencing. When there is no physical boundary to separate our emotional experiences from others' experiences, our experiences start to merge, thus warranting the need for us to set personal boundaries with others (Sweeton, 2019). We must intentionally do this work to establish boundaries with others, unlike our skin that provides that information to our brain automatically and instinctively.

Healthy Brain Functioning in Kids

We want to focus more on working with the body to strengthen (or reregulate) the brain with kids as their frontal lobe is not fully developed, and therefore there is less cortical processing happening in younger brains. So, we need to teach them how to pay attention to their bodies and the way in which their bodies communicate. The prefrontal cortex is not fully developed until around 27 years of age (van der Kolk, 2015; Stixrud and Johnson, 2018; Sweeton, 2019). The child's brain is a more bottom-heavy brain because of this. The lower areas of the brain (the more primitive areas of the brain primed for survival such as the amygdala and insula) are more highly activated, making them more vulnerable to trauma (Sweeton, 2019). During the first months to 2 years of life, the right hemisphere develops, as it is responsible for attachment, attunement, and is primed and ready for attachment, which is critical in the first two years of life (Sweeton, 2019). After the first two years of life, slowly the left hemisphere starts to come online. Language starts to come alive. The amygdala is highly active because they are completely helpless and at mercy of the world (Sweeton, 2019). As they develop and form safe attachments and experience a safe environment, the amygdala calms down. Neurons are pruned off the amygdala, helping it to become more regulated. We need healthy, safe attachments in order to calm the amygdala. The autonomic nervous system (ANS) searches for cues of safety and danger (Sweeton, 2019). The cingulate and prefrontal cortex (PFC) eventually start to develop and come online. Personality solidifies around 30 years of age (Sweeton, 2019).

Trauma in kids is different than trauma in adults (van der Kolk, 2015; Sweeton, 2019). The first two years of life are the most critical for having strong, healthy attachment. Getting needs met facilitates the right hemisphere development, which then facilitates the left hemisphere development. If needs are not met during the first two years, at least 30% of the time, development of the brain slows down, as well as each developmental phase thereafter (Sweeton, 2019). The earlier the disruption of attachment, the more the development of the right hemisphere is disrupted, and therefore the left hemisphere does not develop on time. The long-term effect is an underactive left hemisphere. We become stuck in negative emotions and are prone to engage in withdrawal/avoidance behaviors. According to Dr. Sweeton, there is another critical period for attachment at 5 years old, and again at 10/11 years old. Death of a parent at 9/10 years of age is different than at 11/12 years of age. Kids are vulnerable to trauma as brain development is interrupted.

If the left hemisphere never fully develops, it is likely to result in severe depression as they get older, which is recognized as trauma-based depression. In addition, the amygdala won't prune if they don't have a safe attachment with their caregiver, resulting in an increase in anxiety for life. Other symptoms include a lack of concentration, lack of identity formation, frontal lobe deficits, and lack of connection with others (Sweeton, 2019). You can see how our personal sense of control would be minimal, if anything, if we are not able to develop a sense of identity or connection with others, let alone focus or concentrate on a regular/consistent basis. The less developmental interruptions, the healthier the brain develops.

To help facilitate our kids' brain development, and help recover from past anxiety or trauma, we want to engage them in movement, sensory, and play based objectives (Sweeton, 2019). Movement has everything to do with emotional development. We can do this in a few different ways:

Bottom-up techniques: These are used particularly when we are not able to do the cognitive work to manage our anxiety. We use our body to change the brain. These techniques can include (but are not limited to):

Diaphragmatic breathing

- Reduces amygdala activity and sympathetic nervous system arousal

- Reduces anxiety

- Improves emotional regulation

- Strengthens the Prefrontal cortex

- Reduces insular activity

- By connecting attention to their breath, we increase sensory awareness

- Activates the Vagus Nerve, which then:

    - Hooks directly into the amygdala

    - Activates the Parasympathetic Nervous System

    - Relaxes the body

- Progressive muscle relaxation

  - tense major muscle groups at approx. 40%, intensity for 7 seconds, and relax for 10 seconds

- Exercise

- Yoga

- Mindfulness- Focusing on selected sensations to achieve psychophysiological relaxation

Top-down techniques: These are cognitive exercises, using the brain to re-train itself to strengthen and re-regulate the specific structures of the brain that are affected by anxiety or trauma. These include (but are not limited to):

- Cognitive restructuring/reappraisal

- **Non-avoidance (Restructuring neural networks)**

- Talk therapy (can also be bottom-up)

  - Establishing rapport with students

  - Establishing a meaningful relationship, connection, social re-engaging, forming healthy attachment

- Interpersonal skills training

  - Communication

  - Setting boundaries

- Meditation

Horizontal techniques: These are techniques that work across the left and right hemispheres, activating both hemispheres so they engage with one another, and facilitating the strengthening and activation of core brain structures involved in anxiety. These include (but are not limited to):

- Processing across modalities or hemispheres (bilateral stimulation)

- Art therapy

- Exercising

  - Walking/running

  - Increases sensory awareness—connecting external movement and sensations with internal experiences

  - Bilateral stimulation by walking/running can help aid in calming the limbic system.

These modalities help in teaching self-regulation, improves attention and concentration, and cognitive control.

Add laughter to build healthy neuronal networks.

Should we start with top-down approaches or bottom-up approaches with our students? And why? Bottom-up is used first when a student is not able to identify their anxiety provoking thoughts, are not able to focus, concentrate, or problem-solve. Even if a student is able to focus on managing their anxiety in one area, but then their anxiety spikes again in another area, they may be able to do some of the top-down cognitive work, but their amygdala is still highly activated. Therefore, they need to practice bottom-up exercises to calm the amygdala, in order to do the top-down cognitive work.

Program Success

One of the programs I worked at during my doctoral training was an intensive community-based acute treatment center, the Wetzel Center, in Worcester, Massachusetts. This program was a step-down facility from a hospital, where kids, ranging from ages six to eighteen, were housed and treated when they were discharged from a hospital but were not stable enough to go back into their communities. There were two separate units, one for latency-aged kids (between six and twelve years of age) and an adolescent unit (thirteen through eighteen years of age). During the time I worked there, the Wetzel Center had the lowest recidivism rate for inpatient programs across the state. Other programs, as well as insurance companies, would visit the Wetzel Center to see how they ran their program and to understand why it was more successful than other programs in the state. The state-run health insurance required hospitals to call the Wetzel Center first when stepping a child down to a lower level of care.

However, as well as the Wetzel Center was doing at that time, I was not yet applying my Control Theory in my practice. I was practicing Cognitive Behavioral Theory and Structural Family Theory and using a strength-based approach in my work that I learned from my mentor, Dr. Robert Dingman. Dr. Dingman guided me in my practice with my clients, helping them shift their focus so they were not just recognizing the negative behaviors in which they engaged, but also looking at how frequently they could have engaged in a negative or maladaptive behavior and chose not to. It was a strength-based approach in which we worked with clients to shift their focus from the things they had done wrong to recognizing how successful they had been at exercising healthy control in their lives.

Although we used a strength-based approach with the clients and the Wetzel Center was a top treatment center in the state, it was not actively recognized by the clinical or unit staff that control was something that was at the root of all the work being done at the center. For several years after working at the Wetzel Center, I often thought about and questioned why the Wetzel Center was so successful. As I started focusing on the role of control in my clinical work, specifically studying more about anxiety, I recognized this same theme in the work that was done at the Wetzel Center.

First, there was constant communication. Clinical and unit staff would meet each morning to discuss cases, inform the team of upcoming or potential meetings, and discuss how each client on the units was doing. We also discussed any issues that came up and options for how to manage those issues. Everyone had an important role and participated in the discussion. There was also communication between the clinical staff, unit staff, and the clients' caregivers, outside providers, schools, and other community service providers. The unit staff would constantly communicate with others about how the clients were doing, who had a visit, who was able to go off unit, how they were doing with other clients on the unit, and any upcoming transitions for clients.

Furthermore, before clients were discharged, the unit and clinical staff would schedule appointments with outside providers to make sure they would have follow-up support when they transitioned back into the community. There would also be case conferences for each client within the first week of their admittance and every couple of weeks thereafter, as well as a discharge meeting, to keep all caregivers and treatment and community providers informed on how each child was doing and what the treatment/discharge plan would be as the clients continued to make progress in their work. The Wetzel Center functioned optimally in large part because of its high level of communication within the units and between clinical staff, families, and outside providers.

The clinical work within the units was just as critical as the communication needed to run the units. This work was also successful as a result of the communication between the unit staff and the clients. Granted, the first two weeks after the clients were admitted were typically difficult. It was a stressful transition for the clients at any age. It's understandable that a child would need some time to adjust to a new place and program, but let's look at the role in which control, or the lack thereof, plays in this transition.

When a child (or anyone, for that matter) is new to any type of environment, their personal sense of control is going to be low. The reason is that when they don't know what to expect, they won't be able to prepare themselves well to quell their anxiety. Unknown factors such as where they are going, who will be there (especially if there won't be anyone familiar there), who will be in charge, what will be expected of them, where they will be staying, how long they will be staying, and when they will be able to see their family contribute to their lack of a sense of control. When we don't know what to expect, our automatic thoughts start racing, and we start assuming the worst is going to happen. Because of this, when a child is new to the unit at a treatment center, they often have a hard time acclimating to their new environment until they start to recognize a consistent routine, and their daily life becomes more predictable.

The units provided clients with a consistent routine every day. Clients quickly learned when they would have to wake up, when to eat, when they would be in school, when they would have free time, when they could call their families, when they would have groups, and when they would meet with their clinicians. Their day-to-day life was highly structured. This structure created predictability. The predictability helped them gain a greater sense of control over what they would be doing day to day, hour by hour. For kids who came from unstructured homes or homes with limited means, this structure and predictability helped them know that they would be getting food that day and when they would be getting that food. It wasn't a guessing game as to whether or not they would eat every day. They knew that they would be provided basic necessities, including compassion, support, validation, encouragement, and people who wanted them to feel better and were helping them gain the skills to help themselves.

They were taught accountability. If they started to get frustrated with or to bother other clients, they were told to focus on themselves. They learned that they were not in charge of others and that their job was to focus on their own responsibilities. They learned how to accept what was not within their control. If they made a bad choice on the unit, they were given a consequence of losing a pass off the unit. They were also provided opportunities for restitution after making a bad choice. They learned from these experiences that they were accountable for their own choices, not anyone else. They had to focus on themselves and make the right choices for themselves.

After the first two weeks of a client's stay at the Wetzel Center, their anxiety typically decreased significantly as they knew they were in a safe, structured, and predictable environment. It was actually common for clients not to want to leave the Wetzel Center after having been so successful and having formed such important relationships with each other and the staff. More often than not, these clients had not experienced a healthy friendship or been able to allow themselves to be vulnerable and trust that another adult was going to help take care of them and make sure they had food and a bed to sleep in each night. Many of them didn't know what it was like to have a consistent, structured routine and know that they were going to stay safe each day. When they woke up at the Wetzel Center, they knew they were safe. They felt a sense of control that they hadn't experienced before. It was quite empowering for the clients, as well as for the staff, to watch and see their progress.

Control, with regard to anxiety, was not discussed in any of the work on the unit or within the clinical work, but the Wetzel Center had implemented the necessary and fundamental objectives to help clients gain a healthier sense of control in their lives. There was consistency in the clinical staff, including clinicians, psychiatrists, and directors, as well as the unit staff who were with the clients twenty-four hours a day. Taking all these factors into account, it's not surprising that the Wetzel Center became a leading treatment facility.

Unfortunately, there are numerous facilities that focus on alternative objectives where clients are not learning the necessary skills and awareness of their level of functioning. For example, I've had clients who had previously been diagnosed with eating disorders and have spent time in treatment facilities targeted for eating disorders. The experiences that these clients described were in direct opposition to what they needed in order to exercise control over their disorder or symptoms. Clients are often instructed to make a certain weight before being discharged (needing to be at 80 percent of what their weight should be). The necessity for them to get to a healthy weight can be, and often is, a matter of life and death. However, my clients' clinical progress was not measured. Furthermore, their anxiety was not even discussed in terms of understanding the root cause of their eating disorder.

One client was told to "avoid" thinking about what she was eating and to have her parents control everything she ate. My client was not allowed to eat anything if it did not come from her parents. This approach only increased my client's anxiety as she was instructed to avoid taking responsibility for her disorder. She was not provided appropriate clinical education or treatment objectives to actually get control over her anxiety but was told to give complete control to her parents. This completely enabled the client and placed her responsibilities on her parents, which only led to increased anxiety for both the client and her parents. The client's personal sense of control continued to decrease, increasing anxiety and other symptoms, making her more vulnerable to depression and other, more severe symptoms and destructive thoughts rather than helping her manage her eating disorder.

Now let's take a look at another type of program, Alcoholics Anonymous (AA). Here is a program that, even though not everyone who is battling addiction utilizes it, provides some of the core principles that Control Theory addresses. The most important objective that AA emphasizes is the need to take accountability. In order to work a healthy recovery (not just be sober but actually work their recovery), members have to acknowledge that they don't have control over their addiction. They need to take accountability for their choices and behaviors. This does not just refer to their addiction. As previously discussed, they need to take accountability in all aspects of their life, including relationships (friendships or other), job responsibilities, personal responsibilities, self-care, and other interpersonal situations. Within their recovery, they need to take responsibility for their behaviors that were influenced by their addiction, such as hurting others, risky or impulsive behaviors, or illegal activity. They need to acknowledge that they are personally responsible for the choices they make and for caring for themselves. They cannot be dependent on anyone else to take care of them. Granted, they utilize various support systems, but they are the ones doing the work, not those in their support systems.

Another aspect of AA that Control Theory addresses is accepting what is not within our control. Recovery (which, again, is different from sobriety) happens when we accept that we don't have control, not only over our addiction, but over endless things, including the people in our lives. We have to accept that we are not always going to get what we want. Things aren't always going to go the way we plan. We can't always manipulate people or circumstances in order to get what we want. Once we accept the things over which we don't have control, we are then able to shift our focus to what we *can* do and what *is* within our control.

In the 1970s, psychologist Bruce Alexander (2010) studied the effects of highly addictive drugs on rats. In one setting, rats were confined to solitary steel cages, having no social interaction or playful stimulation of any kind. They were completely isolated. The other setting was a group of rats that were provided with social interaction with other rats and a "rat park" in which they could always play on different apparatuses. They also cohabited with the opposite sex. As a result, baby rat pups joined the mix. These rats were not confined.

Each of these settings provided access to highly addictive drugs, including morphine, heroin, cocaine, and amphetamine, using the press of a lever, otherwise known as a Skinner box. The researchers were able to measure that amount of substances consumed by the rats in each setting. The study found that the rats that were completely isolated consumed significantly more drugs than the rats in the rat park. In fact, there was minimal use of drugs by the rats in the rat park. The researchers concluded that these highly addictive substances were not consumed if the rats were able to engage in a social environment where their activity and social interactions were not restricted.

Applying Control Theory, the rats in the rat park had a higher level of control in their lives than the rats that were in solitary confinement. When there is an increased sense of personal control, anxiety is lower, and there is a decreased likelihood of utilizing other methods (e.g., drugs) to alleviate anxious feelings or increase their sense of control. The rats that had a greater level of control and freedom in their environment were less likely to use the drugs that were readily available to them. (See www.brucealexander.com/articles-speeches/rat-park/148-addiction-the-view-from-rat-park for more information on the study.)

When we feel controlled by outside factors, including people, circumstances, feeling disconnected from others, feeling isolated, trauma, etc., our personal sense of control drops, which automatically increases our anxiety. As our anxiety increases, we become vulnerable to engaging in maladaptive behaviors to alleviate this anxiety, which provides a false sense of control, if we are not aware of this anxiety or how to manage it appropriately. We need to accept the things and circumstances over which we don't have control and then shift our focus to what we *can* do that is within our control. Doing so will allow us to shape our own destiny and gain personal fulfillment and meaning in our lives.

Understanding the Importance of Mental Health Education in Schools and in Law Enforcement: Preventing Tragedies

Approximately one in five students suffers from some symptom of mental illness (American Psychiatric Association, 2016). Anxiety disorders are the most common mental health illness in the United States, affecting forty million adults ages eighteen and older (18 percent of the population) (Anxiety and Depression Association of America, 2015). Only one-third of those suffering receive treatment. Anxiety affects one in eight children (at a clinical level), and when not treated, students are at higher risk for poor school performance, increased maladaptive and risky behaviors, and interference with social functioning (CDC, 2018).

Schools can serve as crucial facilitators in aiding students with education on what mental health is, particularly regarding helping students understand anxiety and the role it plays in their daily lives. Unfortunately, the U.S. education system is more achievement oriented than child oriented. Children need to be empowered to live effectively in the world, independent of their academic achievements. Empowered children will be more resilient and will be able to utilize control in ways that are not maladaptive, but more solution focused.

Teaching students objectives such as anxiety management, stress tolerance, emotional regulation, interpersonal skills, solution-focused work, and being taught how the brain works under anxiety can help prevent them from developing more severe mental health issues or engaging in other maladaptive behaviors. They can utilize these same tools across domains, whether it's managing academics, at home, in social situations, peer pressure, bullying, substance use, or body image issues, and, of course, help them exercise control over their general anxiety.

The result:

- Increased self-esteem/self-confidence

- Increased sense of self/agency

- Increased ability to manage anxiety on a daily basis

- Stronger problem-solving skills

- Learning to take accountability for their choices, actions, and behaviors

- Focusing on themselves and their own responsibilities rather than focusing on others or comparing themselves to others

- Increased interpersonal/communication skills, leading to more positive, healthy relationships

- Increased school attendance

- Decreased avoidance behaviors

- Decreased risky and maladaptive, risky behaviors

By learning how to exercise more control over their anxiety, they will be less likely to use substances to alleviate their anxiety, therefore helping prevent substance use and dependence. Controlling anxiety can aid in preventing or minimizing self-injurious behaviors, including cutting or behaviors that can lead to eating disorders. Knowing how to control anxiety can prevent or decrease the likelihood that students will be bullied or even act as bullies. Students will learn ways to take accountability and understand how they gain more control from taking responsibility for their choices. They will be able to focus on themselves more instead of focusing on what they think others want them to do or comparing themselves to others.

There is clearly a lack of preventative services within school systems. Students need education about mental health before they start to experience severe depression or other mental health issues. It is not enough to help provide support after something extreme happens to an individual student or an entire school. We need to teach students what they can do to take care of themselves before they get to a point of hopelessness or find themselves too deep in a pattern of unhealthy behaviors.

Furthermore, by educating students about anxiety and mental health, we can "normalize" mental health and anxiety. If schools really want to destigmatize mental health issues, it's not enough just to refer students to mental health care providers *after* they have been experiencing extreme anxiety or depression for a prolonged period of time. We need to normalize anxiety. We can help them understand that every single person has anxiety, yet it does not mean that they have a disorder. We want students to understand that nothing is wrong with them if they are feeling anxious, but we want them to have more awareness about their own anxiety. Additionally, if a student continues to feel overwhelmed with anxiety and/or depression, we want them to recognize that they may need additional help and feel that it is OK to reach out for that help. Again, it does not mean that something is wrong with them. Anxiety plays a significant role in our daily lives, and it cannot be emphasized enough that students need to learn what anxiety is and how they can best control it.

Another reason for providing this type of education in schools is that school counselors are overloaded. It is nearly impossible for counselors to provide individual time for all the students who feel they need help. It is also common for students not to recognize when they are overwhelmed with anxiety until their lives start to feel unmanageable, and they may be embarrassed to ask for help. By providing an educational forum for students, we can provide them with a level of insight so they become aware of their anxiety and can start to utilize tools to get control over it. There are too many students who are in need of services and who are not receiving them or the support they need due to the ratio of students to counselors.

Not only is it overwhelming for school counselors and those students who want to be seen, but it can be a burden on the students and families if they are trying to access care outside of the school. Health insurance may not be required to cover mental health treatment down the road, therefore limiting students' (or anyone's, for that matter) access to mental health services in their community. To further complicate the accessibility of mental health services, there are more and more providers practicing out of network with insurance companies, which again limits provider availability when most families are not able to pay out of pocket for these services. If students (and parents) are provided with an educational base on anxiety and mental health, we can help facilitate their getting basic help in managing anxiety to "inoculate" them against falling victim to stressors. It provides an opportunity for students and families to learn how to communicate with each other and how to create a dialogue within their families or with the school about a student's struggles.

Another critical factor that mental health education can work to prevent, or decrease is the likelihood of school refusal. There is a new federal education law (Every Student Succeeds Act, ESSA), which requires schools to measure their success using five particular measures. Four of those measures are strictly based on academic performance, but the law allows the fifth measurement to be decided by the states. At this time, the majority of states are choosing to measure school success by measuring "chronic student absenteeism" (NPR, 2017), which is the most popular nonacademic measurement of school success. However, absenteeism is measured using a statistical measure and not by understanding why students are absent or what prevents them from attending class. Research tends to focus on the prognosis of students who are not attending school, not necessarily what precipitates a student's decision not to attend. Research suggests that students who are "chronically absent" are more likely to fall behind in school and/or drop out completely (Young, 2017). The most recent studies of school absentee rates found that more than 6 million students are "chronically absent," meaning absent more than 10 percent of the total number of days for the school year (NPR, 2017).

Even though there are studies that track the rate of student absenteeism, there are no concrete action plans to address or decrease student absentee rates, other than giving consequences for offenders. Giving students consequences for not attending school is not going to help the students feel supported, understood, or more motivated to attend school and for the right reasons. Nor will these consequences help students feel like they are provided an opportunity to address what is preventing them from attending school. Consequences can actually be more of a deterrent for students than a way of getting them to attend school. For schools to improve their students' success rate, they need to understand what factors prevent students from attending school, provide support for students and their families, and understand why it can be difficult for their students to attend school.

Schools need to identify factors that contribute to students not attending school or poor academic performance. Are they being bullied, having a hard time separating from their parents, afraid of being judged, having other negative experiences at school, or is there a history of trauma? What is their story? All of these situations present dynamics in which a student's sense of control is minimized. Schools need to be aware of the fact that, when students do not feel they have adequate control in certain areas of their lives, they are at an increased risk of missing school. Their anxiety, related to school or not, is likely to be contributing to school avoidance or other maladaptive behaviors.

One other benefit that mental health education in schools can provide is a preventative measure for school violence. We are continuously witnessing acts of violence in schools, especially over the past couple of decades, which seem to be increasing in frequency. By teaching students ways in which they can gain healthy control back in their lives and exercise control in appropriate ways (rather than using control in maladaptive ways), we can help prevent violence. Violence is yet another way in which control is exercised wrongly, which is rooted in anxiety and not having an adequate sense of steering the course of one's life. We need to help our students understand their anxiety and where it comes from and help them gain back healthy control in their lives before hurting the lives of others. Those who engage in violent behavior are not likely to know any other way to successfully manage their anxiety and mental health. Control is the key factor that drives their behavior. Wouldn't you want someone who has access to firearms to have other means of controlling their anxiety and anger, helping prevent them from engaging in violence? I would.

Because mental health is such a significant and broad topic, it's important for students to understand the role anxiety plays in their everyday lives, as well as in their own family dynamics. Whether students come from strained family dynamics, experience extreme anxiety due to academic or social expectations, are being bullied in school, have experienced stressful or abusive relationships, or have a history of trauma, we can help them learn ways to manage these situations, to focus on their needs, and to identify factors over which they have control. Students are more likely to be successful in school when they feel they have more control in other aspects of their lives by having a safe environment to be in and receive support. This does not necessarily mean changing the circumstances that are causing such stress for students but teaching them how to identify and focus on factors over which they *do* have control. We can help them identify options (focusing on solutions) that are more manageable and realistic in exercising control in their stressful environments.

According to the WHO, there is very little financial investment for mental health services. Even in high-income countries like the United States, nearly 50 percent of people suffering from depression are not receiving the help that they need. For every dollar invested in mental health treatment, specifically for anxiety and depression, according to the WHO, there is a return of four dollars (US) in better health and ability to work. In our current state of health care and insurance, insurance companies are required to cover costs for mental health and substance use treatment. However, insurance companies are paying the providers less and less, while subscribers are paying more and more for their coverage and getting minimal benefits. Providers have a hard time keeping up with the cut in their contracted rates and are increasingly discontinuing their participation with insurance panels, which leaves subscribers having to pay more out of pocket for their treatment. This system is critically flawed. Again, this highlights the need for mental health education and preventative work to be provided in the schools, so families won't be stuck having to pay excruciating amounts of money for basic mental health education and support for their children. Also, when people are not able to get the help they need, they oftentimes find themselves struggling to attend school or work, which puts a financial burden on families when a parent is not able to work, either for mental health reasons or because they are taking care of a child who is not able to go to school.

Lastly, Florida recently enacted a law that requires students to provide information on whether they have been referred for mental health services upon registering for school. This is in an effort to identify at-risk students and was prompted after the mass shooting of seventeen students at Marjory Stoneman Douglas High School in February 2018. Four hundred million dollars have also been dedicated to providing mental health resources in Florida public schools. With this money, more psychologists and counselors have been hired to help manage mental health concerns in the schools. However, this approach can be more damaging than it is helpful. First, by providing schools with personal mental health information, students and their families will feel more stigmatized than ever, not to mention that this information will be in the students' permanent records. Students and parents are likely not going to want to provide personal information. Second, mental health information is confidential. Regardless of whether there are resources and mental health professionals available, students are going to be more focused on how they are judged and treated than on accessing help at school. They will continue to feel stigmatized if schools don't address mental health appropriately in an educative and preventative way. Because mental health is as stigmatized as it is, those who suffer from mental health issues, even basic anxiety, are likely going to assume that they are in a different classification than their "normal" peers. Acknowledging mental health issues or the need to reach out for help can be, and often is, interpreted as a weakness or that something is wrong with them. I feel this approach to managing mental health issues in the schools is headed in the absolute wrong direction.

Taking It To The Classroom: A qualitative report on mental health education in schools

Much of my work takes place in school settings, working with students from Kindergarten through college level students. I have been working with schools to implement Social and Emotional Learning programs with the aim of changing the culture of mental health throughout the schools.

I have been observing classes throughout kindergarten through 12th grade, speaking with teachers to assess students' level of functioning in the classroom throughout the pandemic (as well as prior to the pandemic). I have also been listening to teachers' current concerns, presenting to students of all grade levels, teaching students ways to manage their anxiety, presenting to parents on anxiety and mental health, providing professional development training for teachers, and facilitating mental health retreats for the staff throughout the schools.

My focus with the teachers and staff has been to help them understand their students' behaviors versus misinterpreting them. I worked with teachers to facilitate ways in which they can communicate with their students regarding anxiety, track anxiety with their students, take time to engage in play/active exercises to help manage anxiety throughout the day, and help facilitate their students' emotional regulation skills. My approach has been providing an initial education on what is happening neurologically in the brain when we experience anxiety. My goal was to help teachers and staff understand the basic structures and function of the brain when anxiety increases, as well as what happens under chronic anxiety, trauma, and depression, so they have a stronger understanding of what their students may be experiencing and why. I wanted to bring a new perspective to anxiety and mental health to the teachers and staff not only to help increase awareness of anxiety, but to more accurately interpret and understand what students may be experiencing versus assuming a student has "behavioral issues." I also wanted to equip teachers with options that they could use with their students in the moment if a student is struggling with anxiety, without feeling responsible for knowing what to say or playing a "therapist" role to help calm their students. Furthermore, my aim was to equip students with ways in which they can quickly and easily recognize and manage their anxiety in the moment. Therefore, teachers don't take the responsibility on themselves for managing their students' anxiety but are still able to facilitate their work and provide support.

To help students learn these skills, I have been presenting to students of all ages, teaching them what anxiety is, where it comes from, and what we can do to manage it. My goal is to help each student gain a stronger sense of control over their anxiety and circumstances in which they find themselves struggling. My approach with students is also focused on a neurological perspective. I want them to understand the mechanisms behind their anxiety, and ways in which we can strengthen specific structures in the brain to overcome anxiety, trauma, and depression, and to help manage anxiety in healthy and productive ways on a daily basis.

Since the implementation of this work, teachers have been approached by students after the mental health education presentations with additional comments or questions. Students started applying this information to other areas outside of school, such as sports. For example, a high school teacher and coach has been taking the information presented to the teachers, and applying it to not only his classes, but also to his athletes on the football field. The students have then been able to further understand the work their coach has been applying on the field by having a greater understanding of the brain. They are able to pay attention to how they are now helping strengthen specific structures of their brain when engaging in various activities and exercises.

Other key areas of our mental health education include: 1.) how critical sleep is on the brain, and how damaging it is when we don't get enough or quality sleep, and 2.) how critical it is to focus on themselves and not compare themselves to others; making decisions that are right for them or in their own best interest, versus making decisions in order to please others, which takes away from their own personal sense of control.

Another critical, key focus area I address with students, as previously mentioned, is providing education on depression and how we come to be in a state of depression. One of the most important messages I want to instill in students (particularly high school students) is that if they ever reach a state of depression or experience depressive symptoms, including suicidal thoughts, that there is a way out of it. I know it is hard to comprehend if you have ever experienced depression or suicidality, especially after trying to do whatever you can to get out of that feeling and nothing works. But my message is that we CAN get out of it. Our ticket out: tackling anxiety and shifting our personal sense of control back into our hands. When I deliver this message to the students, I can see their reactions. I see their heads nodding along as I take them down the trajectory of prolonged anxiety, and what happens in the brain when we shift from a state of heightened anxiety into a depression. When I talk about how depression comes into play and how easily suicidal thoughts come to the forefront, their heads drop. They know the feeling. They know what I'm talking about. There seems to be an element of shame when I address suicide, but my message to the students is that it's not shameful, but to help them understand what is happening neurologically in the brain; that this is how all of our brains function, and that there are things we can do to undo the damage caused by our anxiety and trauma. I want students to understand that their brain is doing exactly what it needs to do in order to keep us as safe as possible given the stressors or trauma we endure. Nothing is wrong with their brains. But because our defense mechanisms are so adaptive, we go right back into that same defense mechanism the next time our anxiety spikes. Our defense mechanisms therefore become maladaptive when we are no longer unsafe, even though they initially served a purpose to protect us. However, we don't have to live a life with severe, prolonged anxiety and depression. We can actually get control back in our lives. By teaching our students this from an early age, we will help curb the trajectory of where our mental health is heading, and actually build resilience in our students.

Survey Findings

At the start of the SEL program in the schools of one particular district at which I taught, we sent out a survey to students, teachers, and parents to get a baseline assessment to gauge peoples' level of understanding of what anxiety is, where it comes from, how it may be impacting their daily functioning, and how well they feel they manage their anxiety. I am going to present these findings.

At the outset of the SEL program, 28% of those who responded to the survey reported experiencing a daily level of anxiety that was extremely overwhelming, and their cognitive functioning was impaired on a daily basis. Based on the level at which these respondents reported experiencing daily anxiety, the brain is actively engaged in the stress response system, where their prefrontal cortex is compromised. When the prefrontal cortex is compromised, we are not able to (or have a difficult time) focusing, concentrating, communicating effectively, and are in a reactive state. In addition, 38% of the respondents reported experiencing elevated levels of daily anxiety; however, they were still able to manage it.

As far as respondents' level of understanding of anxiety, 81% reported at the outset they felt they had a strong understanding of what anxiety is. However, 90% of those who responded to the survey at the end of the SEL program reported having a clearer understanding of anxiety and where it comes from compared to what they understood at the outset of the program. One of the questions I asked all the students, teachers and parents at the outset was if anyone could give me a definition of anxiety. There wasn't a single person who was able to give me a definition. All responses included a symptom of anxiety. This is why I focus so much on educating everyone on anxiety: it is severely misunderstood, and therefore not treated appropriately. It is extremely rare, in my experience, that anyone who suffers from depression has been assessed for their anxiety. We can't successfully treat depression if we don't treat the underlying root cause- anxiety.

Regarding depression, 82% of the respondents at the start of the program reported feeling they had a strong understanding of what depression is, while 69% reported knowing what causes depression, and 23% reported not knowing what causes depression. After participating in the SEL program, 88% of survey respondents reported having a better understanding of depression and what causes depression compared to what they understood at the start of the program.

One of the most significant areas of focus in my work with students and teachers is assessing how strongly expectations play in an individual's anxiety. This includes whether someone puts expectations on themselves, or if they feel others put expectations onto them, and feeling the pressure to perform or live up to those expectations. At the start of the SEL program, 61% of the survey respondents reported feeling they must meet other peoples' expectations, whether it's regarding academics, social expectations, professional expectations, performance in sports or extracurricular activities, or other personal choices. Furthermore, 80% reported having high expectations of themselves. This is one of the most important areas in my work with anxiety. As students (and adults) are focusing on what others expect of them and make decisions based on what they think others want them to do, they are essentially allowing others to have control over them and their life choices and are not focusing on themselves or what is in their best interest. We need to teach our students to focus on themselves, what is right for them, and what they feel is in their best interest, versus living a life to please others and not feel they have their own sense of control over their choices or a sense of agency. By teaching our students to focus on themselves, we are teaching them how to take accountability for their choices and behaviors. They learn that no one else is making their decisions for them, good or bad, and that their choices are their own. They learn to own their behaviors and choices.

Similarly, 53% of the survey respondents at the outset reported that they frequently make decisions based on what they feel others want them to do, and 60% reported making decisions based on how they want others to view them. This is further evidence that students (and adults) too often focus more on what others want of them or how they want to be perceived, versus focusing on themselves and exercising their own control over what is in their own best interest. To further break this down, I assessed what areas people would like to have a stronger personal sense of control in their lives. When assessing personal control at the start of the program, 60% of the respondents reported wanting to have a stronger sense of personal control in their personal lives, while 53% reported wanting a stronger sense of control in their social lives, and 50% in academics.

After participating in the SEL program, 75% of the respondents reported focusing more on what decisions they need to make for themselves (what is in their own best interest) versus focusing on what others want them to do. However, 66% of the respondents reported still feeling the need to meet others' expectations, whether it's regarding academics, social expectations, performance in sports or extracurriculars, or other personal choices. Ideally, we still want this number to decrease. In addition, 80% of the respondents still have high expectations of themselves. (We would also like this number to decrease). Having ongoing, continuous focus on anxiety management will likely decrease students' needs to please others and condition themselves to make decisions based on what they feel is right for themselves.

At the end of the SEL program, 84% of survey respondents reported feeling they have an increased sense of awareness of when and how they experience anxiety compared to at the start of the program, and 78% reported having increased awareness of how to effectively manage their anxiety in a healthy, productive way. One of the tools that was presented in our work was the anxiety scale to gauge the level of anxiety on a daily basis. According to those who responded to the survey after participating in the program, 44% reported using the anxiety scale on a daily basis to help gauge and keep track of their anxiety on a daily basis. Ideally, I would like the scale to be utilized more to help increase overall personal sense of awareness of anxiety. However, 92% reported feeling confident they can more effectively manage their anxiety compared to 72% at the outset.

Another factor that was assessed at the outset of the SEL program was sleep. According to those who responded to the surveys, 61% reported working on managing a more consistent sleep schedule compared to 53% at the start of the program. As previously mentioned in the reading, sleep plays a vital role in mental health and brain development and is something for which I always assess. When students do not get enough sleep, they are preventing their brain (particularly the prefrontal lobe) from developing the way it needs. This leads to higher levels of anxiety (as quickly as the following day), increased impulsivity and compromised emotional regulation.

This SEL program is a unique program compared to other mental health programs in schools due to the in-depth education and preventative measures used to assess and manage anxiety. I approached this overhaul of the mental health culture with a scientific, psychoneurological approach to help students, teachers and parents understand the root of any mental health issue, and work from the root of the anxiety. I presented a more general and broader picture of anxiety and mental health, as well as focus on the primary goal of each individual person working to gain a stronger personal sense of control, sense of self, and strengthen their overall self-esteem and agency. I then broke the objectives down and applied the neurological components to the clinical components of our work to provide a more thorough, comprehensive understanding of anxiety, depression, and overall mental health.

Standing Apart From Other Programs

Other established school programs that address mental health have not yet expanded into middle or elementary school levels. However, schools are reporting seeing younger and younger students with significant needs (Westport Journal, March 2022). It is often difficult to "convince" students to ask for help when they need it. Oftentimes, they don't realize they may need help and of course, more times than not, are embarrassed to ask for help. By providing mental health education in a classroom setting, where it is part of the curriculum for all students, it helps level the playing field, normalizing the need for support by providing more concrete context around how the brain works, without singling out students. By providing more education on how the brain works regarding anxiety, they are given more context as to why they may struggle from time to time and better understand their own behaviors. By having a stronger understanding, they are less likely to misinterpret their own behaviors and are less likely to have their behaviors misinterpreted by teachers. Kids often misinterpret and assume they are bad kids, a disappointment, a failure or not good enough in some capacity when they react impulsively in an anxiety provoking situation. In these instances, their brain automatically goes into "survival" mode. If they understand more about how the brain works, they have more contexts to draw more accurate conclusions as to why they are responding the way they do (such as reacting impulsively). Instead of assuming they are being "bad" based on their impulsive reaction, they can more easily recognize that their nervous system was overwhelmed, which prevents their frontal lobe from being able to work the way we need. It does not mean they are a bad kid. They learn to recognize when they need to focus on calming their nervous system before reacting, helping them maintain their own sense of control, and feeling confident that they can work through a stressful situation.

The New York Times recently released an article in April of 2022, 'It's Life or Death': The Mental Health Crisis Among U.S. Teens", and released a video, "Worried Sick: A Journey Into The Anxious Teenage Mind" where families were interviewed about their own experiences of depression, suicide, and mental health within their family. One adolescent mentioned that schools talk about "drinking and driving, and don't get pregnant when you're in high school. You're told these things, but they don't tell you, 'if you have panic attacks, this is how you can cope with it." This is exactly my point- this is exactly what I worked on in the schools. I had a middle school student have a panic attack during one of my classes. I had just walked through what is happening in the brain when we have panic attacks and was able to facilitate her work by focusing on helping her calm her nervous system with the understanding of how she is working with specific structures in the brain in the moment. She was able to work her way through the panic attack within just a few minutes, and now has the experience of successfully navigating a panic attack, knowing what she can do the next time she starts to feel her anxiety increase to help prevent another panic attack or better understand what is happening in the brain and more quickly recovering from a panic attack. We look at the panic attack as an area of growth versus incorrectly interpreting it as a weakness or that something is wrong with the student.

A major reason why I feel it is critical to implement mental health education into mainstream education is that there is a lack of services across communities. Although doctor's offices are screening for depression, they don't have the resources to refer their patients for mental health services. This is also another area where anxiety is too often missed, where depression is screened for but not anxiety or trauma history, even though anxiety is the root cause of depression. Between anxiety not being screened for properly and the lack of services, students (and parents) are left to their own devices and the anxiety and depression continue to increase to intolerable levels. According to the National Institute of Mental Health, of the three million American adolescents who experienced major depression in 2020, almost two-thirds received no treatment.

A recent study published in the *Journal of Affective Disorders* found that about a third of child suicides occur seemingly without warning and without any predictive signs, such as a mental-health diagnosis, though sometimes a retrospective analysis points to signs that were simply missed. This goes back to my point that if we provide more accurate and preventable mental health education in schools, we can help decrease and prevent child suicides, or at least increase awareness of a child's anxiety that could potentially lead to depression or suicidal ideations. We can provide support for students to help prevent the potential trajectory of anxiety, trauma, or depression, without relying on the need for additional outside mental health providers. Suicide is not as unpredictable as many believe it is if we have the proper education. When a child's frontal lobe is compromised (when the nervous system is overwhelmed, and the stress response system is activated), there is an increased risk for them to act on a suicidal thought. However, if they are taught what is happening in the brain and understand/have more awareness of what is happening in the brain in those overwhelming moments and have a plan of what they can do to manage their nervous system before acting impulsively, they can stop themselves from acting on those thoughts.

In 2020, according to the Centers for Disease Control and Prevention, suicide claimed the lives of more than 500 children in the United States between the ages of 10 and 14, and of 6,000 young adults between 15 and 24 years of age. In the former group, it was the second leading cause of death (behind unintentional injury). This makes it as common a cause of death as car crashes. Innumerable treatments have been proposed for reducing suicide rates. Most have had sporadic success, but none has significantly reduced the scale of the problem. Families/parents often report they are unaware of how their child(ren) is feeling or the state of their mental health. This highlights the need for mental health education for parents as well as for students. Mental health education in the community would not only help prevent further struggles with mental health, but also help parents understand how their children might be getting to a state of strained mental health.

These statistics are further evidence of the need for mental health education in schools, beyond the surface level. Schools need to take action to change the culture of mental health by providing more context behind the workings of the brain, normalizing mental health for each student, teacher, and parent. We can't afford to wait until a student is struggling or in a state of depression to act. We aren't doing our students any good by letting them flounder until something bad happens to them in order to then get them help. We aren't allowing them the opportunity to learn and gain awareness of their own mental health, let alone to train their brain to become more resilient. The more we help them strengthen their brains, the more equipped they will be to overcome anxiety and traumatic experiences in the future. In other words, we are inoculating our kids to help them strengthen, restore, and maintain healthy mental health.

Dr. Bessel Van Der Kolk provides an exceptional description as to why mental health education should be in schools, which is also reflective of my experience in teaching this in schools. He states, "The greatest hope for traumatized, abused, and neglected children is to receive a good education in schools where they are seen and known, where they learn to regulate themselves, and where they can develop a sense of agency. At their best, schools can function as islands of safety in a chaotic world. They can teach children how their bodies and brains work and how they can understand and deal with their emotions. Schools can play a significant role in instilling the resilience necessary to deal with the traumas of neighborhoods or families. But if children feel abandoned, worthless, or invisible, nothing seems to matter. Fear destroys curiosity and playfulness. In order to have a healthy society, we must raise children who can safely play and learn. Teachers' perspectives begin to change when they realize that their students' disturbing behaviors started out as frustrated attempts to communicate distress and as misguided attempts to survive. More than anything else, being able to feel safe with other people defines mental health; safe connections are fundamental to meaningful and satisfying lives. The critical challenge in a classroom setting is to foster reciprocity: truly hearing and being heard; really seeing and being seen by others. We want to translate brain science into everyday practice."

In addition to providing mental health education in schools, I am striving to broaden this work into the field of law enforcement. As I have been designated as the psychologist for police officers in Bergen County, New Jersey, both for individual and professional consultation, I have been focusing on educating police officers on how the brain works under duress, and to help educate them on anxiety and trauma on the brain. My hope is to help officers engage with their citizens in a way where they understand and connect with their citizen's nervous system, to allow the citizen to de-escalate and then re-engage in a productive, controlled manner, facilitating communication. We need to connect with others on a neurological level versus becoming reactive. Just like in clinical practice, police officers need their citizens to meet their level of calm, not for them to meet their citizen's level of chaos. If the officers are reacting to the anxiety and chaos, the citizens will become more defensive as their anxiety quickly increases. Just like all of us, at that point of confrontation, their brain in going to go into survival mode. I feel like we need to approach others with the understanding that they likely have some kind of trauma history, and they aren't choosing to become reactive or aggressive, but their brain goes into survival mode and chooses for them as a means of protection. Trauma develops from secret events that people live, in large part, by themselves. Police officers are not going to have that information on hand and need to assume there is a high likelihood of trauma playing a role in the citizen's mental health and behaviors.

It's important to also understand the correlation between substance use and trauma. According to Dr. Bessel van der Kolk, those who are addicted are likely to have some kind of trauma. Addiction is a physical indication that something isn't right on an emotional level. The relationship with your body is an underlying factor behind drug abuse, self-injurious behaviors, and poor eating behaviors. If law enforcement officers understand substance use in a larger context, they are more likely to effectively engage with citizens. I mention this because children do not "outgrow" their childhood experiences/trauma/abuse. Child abuse is the most significant traumatic precipitant to depression (54%), suicide attempts (58%), alcoholism (78%), sexual assault victims (62%), and domestic violence victims (52%). It is a public health emergency. As Dr. van der Kolk states, we need to create public systems to allow for children to be seen, heard, and cared for, because these kids become adults and their trauma manifests into so much more and is easily misinterpreted and managed in ways that are much more damaging than good. The way in which police officers engage with citizens can play a significant role in creating a safer public system, along with schools.

Another aspect of my work with police officers is to help them process what they witness and experience on a daily basis that is traumatizing in and of itself. My goal is to help them understand, again, how the brain works regarding their own mental health, and to help them separate themselves from their work. This is a field of work where the brain can turn off "work mode" and they can go home to relax for the rest of the day/evening. They need to train their brain how to re-settle the nervous system, engage their PNS to bring them back to homeostasis, and for their brain to recognize that the trauma they witnessed or experienced during their work is over, and that they are safe.

One other aspect of training police officers about the neurobiology of the brain is to help them understand what happens when a victim or an officer is asked to recall information about a traumatic event.

We need to acknowledge the toll trauma takes on the brain, particularly with memory, interpretation, and logical reasoning. We can't rely on the brain to provide completely accurate information under testimony.

You can see how critical it is to better educate ourselves and communities about mental health, particularly on anxiety and trauma. We can't be making assumptions about others without knowing their stories.

Cognitive Behavioral Objectives

Here is a review and an outline of the cognitive objectives that are addressed in Control Theory. These objectives can be applied to a school curriculum focusing on anxiety management and mental health education.[1]

1. *Emotional regulation:* Here is where we work to increase awareness of emotions; provide education on what anxiety is, how it is manifested, and where it is originally rooted; and understand why/when anxiety is likely to be triggered. When we are able to recognize the thought patterns that trigger anxiety, we increase our level of insight into our thought processes and emotions and are therefore better able to recognize ways in which we can control our anxiety as opposed to allowing our anxiety to control our thoughts and behaviors.

2. *Interpersonal skills:* These focus primarily on communication skills; setting personal boundaries; setting limits with others; focusing on ourselves; taking accountability for our own actions and choices; and being able to hold others accountable for their own behaviors, choices, and anxieties. Communication is one of the most important tools we can utilize to increase our sense of control and effectively help lower another person's anxiety and increase their sense of control if we are communicating appropriately with one another and, more specifically, taking accountability for our actions.

3. *Stress tolerance:* Stress tolerance helps teach us how to accept what we don't have control over, how to shift our focus to what *is* within our control, and how to recognize what our priorities are and what we need to be focusing on in the moment. In addition to helping students understand the role of control in anxiety, we address planning, organization, and time-management skills to help students learn how to prioritize their responsibilities and manage their time more effectively, which ultimately is another way in which students learn accountability and responsibility.

4. *Solution-focused work:* Solution-focused work includes cognitive-based objectives to help students and adults stay focused on themselves while learning to work through stressors/anxieties. It promotes flexibility in thinking (as opposed to maintaining rigid thinking, which increases anxiety), problem-solving skills, accountability, responsibility, and learning ways in which we can exercise healthy and appropriate control in stressful circumstances.

---

1 These strategies are also applicable for students who have ADHD or autism diagnoses.

Review of Curriculum Goals Regarding Anxiety Management and Mental Health Education

1. Provide students with a supportive and safe environment where they able to form safe relationships with their teachers.

2. Help students understand what mental health means; help normalize anxiety and other symptoms of our mental health. If schools really want to be "stigma free" when it comes to mental health, we need to normalize anxiety and mental health for our students.

3. Teach students the basics of how the brain works under anxiety and trauma, with the understanding, while teaching them ways to work with their anxiety, rather than becoming consumed by it.

4. Increase understanding of the relationship between anxiety, depression, and suicidal ideations.

5. Increase understanding of how anxiety affects behaviors (including maladaptive, self-injurious, manipulative, aggressive, impulsive, and avoidant behaviors) and ways to help decrease or prevent these behaviors.

6. Increase understanding of the relationship between anxiety and substance use and addiction, and how to help decrease or prevent substance use.

7. Increase understanding of the relationship between anxiety and bullying and ways to help decrease or prevent bullying for both the victim and the aggressor.

8. Increase understanding of the relationship between anxiety and school avoidance and ways to help decrease or prevent school avoidance while still holding students (and parents) accountable.

9. Provide ways to communicate with students when anxiety is recognized while still holding them accountable for their responsibilities and teach students how to communicate effectively with others.

10. Help students understand what is within their control while help-

ing them accept what is not within their control and learn how to focus on themselves and their own responsibilities.

Incorporating Our Tools

Let's incorporate what we have discussed in our reading and apply the specific steps to help us exercise the control on which we've been focusing. The following outline provides a cognitive approach to managing anxiety in the moment where the anxiety is not yet overwhelming to the point of activating the SRS.

1. Identify the stressor/triggering circumstance and level of anxiety.

   - Identify contributing stressful factors.

   - Identify where your anxiety is on a scale of 1 to 10.

   - If your anxiety is at an 8, 9, or 10 on the scale, take space from the triggering situation. Your *only* job when you are this high on the scale is to engage in something to help you calm yourself, such as going for a walk, listening to music, stepping outside, drawing, yoga, or meditation. This does *not* include using alcohol or other substances.

Once you have come down to a 7 or lower on the scale, continue with the following steps.

2. Identify automatic thoughts.

   - Review thoughts to see if they are valid or not.

   - Is there any evidence that these automatic thoughts are *absolutely* true or that they are *definitely* going to happen?

3. Shift your focus to what you are doing in the moment.

   - What is your priority in the moment?

   - What is your responsibility right now?

   - Focus on one task at a time.

4. If your automatic thoughts could be valid:

- Identify options for managing the potential stressor as best you can.

- What is plan A? Plan B? Plan C? (Problem-solving)

- Put the plan aside and shift your focus back to what you are doing in the moment.

5. Practice recognizing and accepting what is not within your control.

6. Shift your focus to what *is* within your control.

- Again, identify or review what your options are, given the circumstances.

- What is plan A? Plan B? Plan C? (Continue with problem-solving.)

7. Communication.

- Communicate any assumptions or anticipatory thoughts (automatic thoughts) with those involved or of concern.

- Validate others' concerns and feelings.

- Set limits/boundaries with others if needed. (Validation of others before setting limits can be very helpful in deescalating the situation as well.)

- Hold others accountable for their own actions or choices, not taking on their responsibilities or anxieties.

- It's OK to tell others that you are not able to help them if you are already feeling overwhelmed by your own responsibilities.

- Tell others to "focus on yourself" if feeling controlled or overpowered by others. Remember that you are in control of yourself. Others do not have control of you.

- Give choices to others when holding them accountable for their behaviors. Put the responsibility onto them rather than trying to control them or engaging in a power struggle.

8. Focus on yourself.

- What are your own responsibilities?

- What are your own priorities? (Not what others want you to prioritize.)

- Make decisions that are in *your* best interest (not in the interest of others). Your job is not to act in ways to please others and meet their needs, especially in an effort to avoid having others become upset. Your job is to focus on making decisions that are in your own best interest. Granted, your intention is never to hurt, disrespect, or offend others. However, you need to work on accepting that others may not agree or be happy with your decisions or even have the same opinions, but others also have to accept that they don't have control over everyone else.

- Again, you can validate what others want from you or how they feel, but then set your limits and stay focused on what is in your own best interest.

- Recognize that you are in control of yourself. Others are not in control of the decisions you make. (There are exceptions here for caregiver-child dynamics, including teacher-child dynamics.)

9. Take accountability for your own choices and behaviors.

- You are not perfect and are bound to make mistakes or poor choices now and then. The important factor on which to focus is how you handle your mistakes. Do you blame others and justify your behaviors, or do you take accountability for your choices and actions?

10. Recognize mental boundaries for yourself.

- Focus on the fact that you are not doing anything wrong (especially when setting limits with others even if they don't like it) and that you are following through with your own responsibilities.

- When you attend to your own responsibilities, you are

doing your job.

- Recognize when your anxiety ends and when the anxiety you might be experiencing is likely someone else's anxiety. Ask yourself, "Is this *my* responsibility?" Again, focus on what your own responsibilities are and be careful not to take on someone else's responsibilities or anxiety.

11. Practice flexibility in thinking.

- Break tasks down into smaller parts, breaking the "all-or-nothing" thinking pattern:

    - Engage in a task for ten to fifteen minutes at a time, then reevaluate how you feel.

    - Study for half an hour, take a break, go back to studying for half an hour, take a break.

    - Accomplish one objective at a time.

        - For example, when struggling to get out of bed in the morning, first focus on getting out of bed and getting to the bathroom. Then reevaluate how you feel. If you need to rest a little more, rest for a little bit and then attempt to get up again. You've already shown yourself that you are capable of accomplishing this. If you feel you are OK, focus on the next task of getting dressed. Then reevaluate how you feel again.

            These objectives also help with focus and concentration, making tasks more manageable rather than your feeling completely overwhelmed.

- Utilize time management.

- Use a daily planner.

- Modify plans as needed when something changes. Identify other times when you can get work done. If you can't do what you were planning to do in the moment, when else can you do it? (This also helps with preventing procrastination.)

12. Reevaluate your anxiety on the scale.

  - Has it decreased after taking these steps?

  - Do you feel an increase in your sense of control? Maybe even a sense of relief? Pride?

13. Do a daily/nightly self-check-in, identifying anything you made progress with that day, any accomplishments, successes, goals met, et cetera.

Examples of accomplishments:

  - Getting out of bed in the morning.

  - Eating.

  - Making it to class or work.

  - Making it to the gym when you had little to no motivation.

  - Going to a doctor's appointment when you really didn't want to.

  - Taking a test that you were dreading.

Other Exercises:

  o One Feared Thing:
    ▪ Step outside your comfort zone once/day to slightly activate the amygdala and to experience the nervous system recovering after engaging in the task, surviving the experience. This helps train the brain to learn self-efficacy.

  o Relaxation technique for anxiety:

    ▪ Practice a relaxation exercise for one minute. Stop. Practice again for one minute. Stop. Practice for one more minute. Stop, then close your eyes and practice for one minute, and repeat. Try to eventually extend the relaxation time.

What Can Parents Do?

- Learn what your anxiety feels like physically and mentally. How is your anxiety manifested? What helps you manage your anxiety to regulate your nervous system?

- Prioritize your health. You need to prioritize your own health and be able to understand and appropriately control your own anxiety to be able to help or understand your children's anxiety.

- Communicate with your kids. Open the line of communication and help teach them that by communicating, they are able to utilize the greatest means of control.

- Validate your child's feelings and concerns. You might not agree with how they feel, but what they experience, whether it's their feelings or how they interpret a situation, is real for them. Don't minimize their experience. You wouldn't want your own experiences to be minimized or disregarded. If you want your children to talk with you and be honest, you have to validate and respect their feelings and experiences.

- Pull back on the level of control as kids get older and more independent. Relinquish some control (where appropriate) so they can exercise more control for themselves. Let your kids make mistakes. Let them fail. Kids will learn more from their failures than if they are micromanaged by parents at ages when they need to learn how to act and make decisions more independently. Kids have to learn how to accept that they are not going to be 100 percent successful at everything they pursue. That's an unrealistic expectation that should not be put onto our kids. It's OK to fail, and kids grow from failure when provided guidance and education on how to understand failure and to learn what they can do moving forward (i.e., taking accountability and problem-solving). Kids won't learn to solve problems when they are enabled by being micromanaged beyond what is appropriate for their age and development. As parents, you need to communicate with your children effectively and hold them accountable for their own choices and actions, but you can't try to control their every move. Some questions to think about include:

- How do your kids handle a situation in which they fail?
  - Do they blame others?
  - Do they make excuses?
  - Do they justify their actions or decisions?
  - Do they take accountability for their own choices?
- How do *you* handle failure?
- What do you think your kids learn from you?

Talk about choices, risk-taking, and natural consequences. Some risk is OK and sometimes necessary to help kids learn what they are capable of accomplishing while simultaneously understanding their limits. For example, if your child chooses not to do their homework or put effort into their classes, they are then choosing to face the natural consequence of not getting a good grade or potentially failing their classes.

- Don't always tell your child what to do in stressful situations but support them by validating their feelings and facilitate the conversation by asking questions about what they have thought of doing, what they have already tried, who they can talk to, what their options might be, et cetera. By facilitating the conversation, you are helping them learn and practice their problem-solving skills. You are helping them build up their own personal sense of control as well as their confidence that they will be able to manage future stressors more successfully.

- Teach kids interpersonal skills such as communication and setting limits with others. Help them understand that others, their peers in particular, do not have control over them. They are in control of themselves. (There are exceptions when parents are in control of their kids, particularly when they are younger, as well as other adult figures in appropriate circumstances, such as a teacher, school personnel, or a supervisor at a job). Teach your kids that they are in control of the choices they make, whether they are good or bad. It is their independent choice to follow through with their responsibilities across different settings. If they choose to not follow through with these responsibilities, they are choosing the natural consequences of their actions. Those choices are under their control. Even if an adult or authoritative figure is speaking to them inappropriately, they can still set a limit with that person, stating they are willing to speak with the adult, but the adult is not to speak to them disrespectfully.

- Help them understand that they don't have control over everything and not everything is going to go their way.

- Teach them to focus on themselves. Focusing on others takes away their personal sense of control. We tend to shift our control to others by allowing others to maintain our attention, neglecting ourselves and preventing us from focusing on what our priority is in the moment or what is currently in our best interests. Kids need to focus on the control they have for themselves rather than comparing themselves to their peers or making decisions based on what others want from them or think they should or should not do. Help them strengthen their own sense of self.

- Don't accommodate avoidant behaviors. Don't enable them by doing things for them. For example, don't do their homework for them, don't allow them to skip school when they don't want to go, and don't talk to your high school or college student's teachers for them when the student needs to be communicating with their teachers themselves. Facilitate a dialogue/communication by asking them guided questions to help them think about what they can do. Help them do the problem-solving without doing the work yourself. You can still support your kids while at the same time holding them accountable for their own responsibilities.

- Help them understand the importance of regulating social media, again emphasizing the importance of focusing on themselves.

- Model appropriate use of phones, iPads, and other devices as parents. Have consistent time away from devices to help teach your kids appropriate boundaries between the virtual and real worlds.

- Teach them about the importance of sleep and help them establish and maintain a consistent sleep-wake cycle.

- Support their need to prioritize sleep over homework. Sleep is critical to helping manage anxiety and depression and should not be neglected in order to get homework done.

- Other sleep tips: keep bedrooms cool, don't exercise within four hours of bedtime, keep the weekend sleep-ins to no more than sixty minutes of additional rest.

- Teach them accountability. Kids need to learn they are responsible and accountable for their own choices. Do not enable your kids by trying to "fix" their issues/stressors by taking control of the situation yourself. When kids learn how to take responsibility for themselves, they are increasing their sense of control as well as their self-confidence.

- The power of a hug: if you don't know what to say in a given moment when your child is hurting or overwhelmed, give them a hug. You don't need to say a word. Just give your child a hug. (Hugging also activates the vagus nerve, helping the nervous system settle down and helps the body feel safe.)

We need to help our kids develop internal motivation by allowing them to exercise more control. Naturally, as parents, we want to make things right for our kids and fix their problems. However, the more of our children's responsibilities we take on as parents, especially as they get older, the less likely our kids will be able to develop their own internal motivation or learn how to exercise control in stressful circumstances. Sometimes we need to allow our kids to fail. We need to help them learn what they can do differently in the future and recognize that their own choices have natural consequences and no one else is to blame. They need to understand the importance of accountability. The more we try to control our kids, the more they will push back and the less willing they will be to hear us as parents and apply what we teach. To reiterate a message by Dr. Stixrud, we need to immunize our children against more potentially damaging mental health issues in the future and to prepare them for happy, healthy, productive lives.

Acknowledgments

I would like to thank the people who have been an incredible support throughout the process of writing my book as well as helping promote my work in the field. I have been very fortunate to have worked with, known, and interacted with so many influential people who have been a driving force for my work.

I want to thank each and every one of my clients throughout my years of practice for providing insight and helping guide my work in cultivating Control Theory. I have learned immensely from my clients and continue to do so each day. I hope that each person with whom I have worked has been able to walk away from our sessions with a clearer understanding of their anxiety and to shift healthy control back into their lives. I hope that each of our sessions left you with having had a positive experience.

I would like to thank my husband for his unending support both in my clinical and public work and throughout the process of writing this book. I would also like to thank my sons, Andrew and Carter, for helping me navigate and master my own treatment objectives! I hope you will both see the benefits of our work in the years to come . . .

I want to say thank you to my professors along the way and, in particular, my mentor, Dr. Robert Dingman. I can't express my gratitude to you for teaching, guiding, and supporting me in my work as I transitioned through different stages of my career. Whenever I start to feel settled in my work, I always remind myself of your words and ask myself, "What's next?" Your words have continued to challenge me every day.

I want to express my gratitude to Emily Bratten for taking time to skillfully review my material and for providing more depth to the messages this book aims to address. Your insight and understanding of this subject have been incredibly valuable.

I would like to thank Dr. William Stixrud for helping guide me in this important subject, for allowing me to use your work as a significant reference, and for your support and guidance in producing my book.

I am grateful for my friends and community supporting my work and pushing to get mental health awareness into our schools. Thank you for being advocates for our children and promoting the need for mental health education in our schools.

Last, but definitely not least, my grandfather, Frank Claybourne, has been a significantly influential hero to me. He has been a pioneer in trying to help adolescents who have been incarcerated receive the treatment they need to help them become successful members of their communities. His advanced thinking paved the way for me to carry out his (and my) vision of providing appropriate treatment and resources for our youth.

References

Ainsworth, M.D.S. (1978). *Patterns of Attachment: a psychological study of the strange situation*. New York: Lawrence Erlbaum Associates.

All Things Considered (National Public Radio). (2017). *A Reformed White Nationalist Speaks Out on Charlottesville*. https://www.npr.org/2017/08/13/543259499/a-reformed-white-nationalist-speaks-out-on-charlottesville

Anxiety and Depression Association of America. (2015). *Facts and Statistics*. https://adaa.org/about-adaa/press-room/facts-statistics

Alexander, B. K. (2010). *Addiction: The View from the Rat Park*. www.brucealexander.com/articles-speeches/rat-park/148-addiction-the-view-from-rat-park

American Psychiatric Association. (2016). *Diagnostic and Statistical Manual of Mental Disorders, Fifth Edition*. Washington, DC: American Psychiatric Publishing.

American Psychological Association. (2011). *The Road to Resilience*. Brochure. Washington, DC: American Psychological Association. www.apa.org/helpcenter/road-resilience.aspx

Beck, A. T. (1976). *Cognitive Therapy and the Emotional Disorders*. New York: International Universities Press, Inc.

Beck, A.T., Wright, F.W., Newman, C. F., & Liese, B. (1993). *Cognitive Therapy of Substance Abuse*. New York: Guilford Press.

Beck Institute. (2018). *Get Informed*. https://beckinstitute.org/get-informed/social-stream

Beck, J. S. (1995) *Cognitive Behavior Therapy: Basics and Beyond*. New York: Guilford Press.

Bowlby, J. (1973). *Attachment and Loss. Vol. 2: Separation: anxiety and anger*. New York, NY. Basic Books.

Bowlby, J. (1982). *Attachment and Loss: retrospect and prospect.* American Journal of Orthopsychiatry, 52 (4), 664-678.

Breus. M. J. "Exercise and Its Benefits for Sleep." *Psychology Today*, September 6, 2017. https://www.psychologytoday.com/us/blog/sleep-newzzz/201709/exercise-and-its-benefits-sleep

Centers for Disease Control and Prevention. (2021). *Disparities in Suicide*. https://cdc.gov/suicide/facts/disparities-in-suicide.html

Centers for Disease Control and Prevention. (2018). *Key Findings: U.S. Children with Diagnosed Anxiety and Depression.* https://www.cdc.gov//childrensmentalhealth/features/anxiety-and-depression.html

Centers for Disease Control and Prevention. (2018). *Suicide Rising across the US.* https://www.cdc.gov/vitalsigns/suicide

Centers for Disease Control and Prevention. (2011, 2013). *Welcome to WISQARS.* http://cdc.gov/injury/wisqars/index/html

Centers for Disease Control and Prevention. (2017). *Leading Causes of Death Reports 1981-2017.* https://webappa.cdc.gov/sasweb/ncipc/leadcause.html

EMDR Institute, Inc. (2019). *What is EMDR?* https://www.emdr.com/what-is-emdr

Flora, C. "The Hardest Word." *Psychology Today*, October 2017, 53–56.

Foxman, P. (2007). *Dancing With Fear: Controlling Stress and Creating a Life Beyond Panic and Anxiety*. Alameda, CA: Hunter House Inc. Publishers.

Green, S. *"Florida Law Requiring Students to Inform School Districts on Mental Health History Is Problematic,"* Orlando Sentinel, August 9, 2018. https://www.orlandosentinel.com/opinion/audience/shannon-green/os-ae-school-districts-mental-health-law-20180809-story.html

Joelson, R. B. *"Locus of Control: How Do We Determine Our Successes and Failures?"* Psychology Today, August 2, 2017. https://www.psychologytoday.com/us/blog/moments-matter/201708/locus-control

Journal of Affective Disorders. (2020). *Suicide in children and young people: can it happen without warning?* Volume 275, October 2020, 307-310.

Kann, L., Kinchen, S., Shanklin, S., Flint, K. H., Hawkins, J., Harris, W. A., Lowry, R., Olsen, E. O., McManus, T., Chyen, D., Whittle, L., Taylor, E., Demissie, Z., Brener, N., Thornton, J., Moore, J., & Zaza, S. (2013). "Youth Risk Behavior Surveillance: United States, 2013." *Morbidity and Mortality Weekly Report* 67(8): 1–114. Published online June 15, 2018. doi: 10.15585/mmwr.ss6708a1

Lambert, C. "*Deep into Sleep.*" Harvard Magazine, July–August 2005. https://harvardmagazine.com/2005/07/deep-into-sleep.html

Linehan, M. M. (1993). *Cognitive-Behavioral Treatment of Borderline Personality Disorder*. New York: The Guilford Press.

Margalit, L. *"What Screen Time Can Really Do to Your Kids' Brains."* *Psychology Today*, April 17, 2016. https://www.psychologytoday.com/us/blog/behind-online-behavior/201604/what-screen-time-can-really-do-kids-brains

Mate, Gabor. (2022). *The Wisdom of Trauma Film*. https://www.thewisdomoftrauma.com

McEwen, B., & Karatsoreos, I. (2015). "*Sleep Deprivation and Circadian Disruption." Sleep Medicine Clinics* 10. https://www.researchgate.net/publication/272892924_Sleep_Deprivation_and_Circadian_Disruption

National Institutes of Mental Health. (2019). *Suicide is a Leading Cause of Death in the United States*. https://www.nimh.nih.gov/health/statistics/suicide.shtml

How Learning Happens (National Public Radio Ed). (2017). *Most States Plan to Use Student Absences to Measure School Success*. https://www.npr.org/sections/ed/2017/09/26/550686419/majority-of-states-plan-to-use-chronic-absence-to-measure-schools-success

New York Times. (2022). *It's Life of Death: the mental health crisis among U.S. teens*. https://www.nytimes.com/2022/04/23/health/mental-health-crisis-teens.html

New York Times (2022). *Worried Sick: a journey into the anxious teenage mind*. https://www.nytimes.com/video/science/100000007871187/mental-health-pandemic-teens.html

National Sleep Foundation. (2017). *Beverages to Avoid to Sleep Soundly While Traveling*. https://www.sleepfoundation.org/sleep-topics/beverages-avoid-sleep-soundly-while-traveling

National Sleep Foundation. (2017). *Children's Stress and Sleep*. https://

www.sleepfoundation.org/sleep-topics/childrens-stress-sleep

National Sleep Foundation. (2018). *How Blue Light Affects Kids and Sleep.* https://www.sleepfoundation.org/sleep-topics/how-blue-light-affects-kids-sleep

National Sleep Foundation. (2018). *Teens and Sleep.* https://www.sleep-foundation.org/sleep-topics/teens-and-sleep

Psychology Today. (2017). *Bullying.* https://www.psychologytoday.com/basics/bullying

Roberts Stoler, D. *"Restorative Sleep Is Vital to Brain Health.* Psychology Today, April 6, 2017. https://psychologytoday.com/us/blog/the-resilient-brain/201704/restorative-sleep-is-vital-brain-health

Scutti, S. *US Suicide Rates Increased More Than 25% Since 1999, CDC Says.* CNN, June 7, 2018. Last updated June 22, 2018. https://www.cnn.com/2018/06/07/health/suicide-report-cdc/index.html

Substance Abuse and Mental Health Services Administration. (2014). *Results from 2013 National Survey on Drug Use and Health: Mental Health Findings*, NSDUH Series H-49, HHS Publication No. (SMA) 14-4887. Rockville, MD: Substance Abuse and Mental Health Services. https://www.samhsa.gov/data/sites/default/files/NSDUHmhfr2013/NSDUHmhfr2013.pdf

Stixrud, W., & Johnson, N. (2018). *The Self-Driven Child: The Science and Sense of Giving Your Kids More Control over Their Lives.* New York: Viking.

Sweeton, J. (2021). *Brain-Based Trauma Therapy.* Mind Works Consulting and Psychological Services, PLLC.

Twenge, J. (2017). *iGen.* New York: Atria Books.

Van der Kolk, B. (2015). *The Body Keeps the Score.* New York: Penguin Books.

Westport Journal. (2022). *Program addressing student mental health issues gets high marks.* Westportjournal.com/education/program-addressing-student-mental-health-issues-gets-high-marks/

World Health Organization (2017). *"Depression: Let's Talk," Says WHO, as Depression Tops List of Causes of Ill Health.* https://www.who.int/en/news-room/detail/30-03-2017--depression-let-s-talk-says-who-as-depression-tops-list-of-causes-of-ill-health

Yale News. "Bullying-Suicide Link Explored in New Study by Researchers at Yale," July 16, 2008. https://news.yale.edu/2008/07/16/bullying-suicide-link-explored-new-study-researchers-yale

Young, J. L. *"Understanding School Refusal: What Parents Need to Know at Back-to-School Time." Psychology Today*, September 11, 2017. https://www.psychologytoday.com/us/blog/when-your-adult-child-breaks-your-heart/201709/understanding-school-refusal

About the Author

Dr. Jolene Arasz is a practicing psychologist and lead certified trauma specialist in northern New Jersey. Her clinical focus is on anxiety and trauma. Dr. Arasz received a dual degree in psychobiology from Albright College in 2002. From there, she attended the Massachusetts School of Professional Psychology to earn her doctoral degree in clinical psychology. Throughout her doctoral education, she did clinical training in various settings, including outpatient services for adults with major mental illness, elementary and middle school systems, the Boston Juvenile Court Clinic, and did inpatient and outpatient work with the agency Y.O.U. Inc. in Worcester, Massachusetts. She continued her postdoctoral training with Y.O.U. Inc., laying the foundation for much of the clinical work she continues today. There, Dr. Arasz worked with children between the ages of six and eighteen, providing intensive individual, group, and family therapy in an inpatient setting for highly traumatized patients. From there, she became the clinical director of a substance abuse treatment center for those who were homeless and fighting addiction, while continuing to provide outpatient services for children, adolescents, and families.

Dr. Arasz currently has a private practice working with adolescents, adults, and families. She is a lead certified trauma specialist, and focuses on anxiety management and trauma treatment by providing a psychoneurological, educational approach to her work in conjunction with Cognitive Behavioral Therapy (CBT) and Eye Movement Desensitization and Reprocessing (EMDR).

Outside of her practice, Dr. Arasz consults with schools, providing professional development training to teachers and school personnel to change the culture of mental health. Dr. Arasz also teaches students, K-12 grades, and speaks at colleges about anxiety and mental health, specifically with a neurobiological focus on anxiety and mental health. This approach is significantly different from other mental health education programs in schools, providing a preventative approach that allows for students to develop adaptive ways of managing anxiety, and therefore preventing them from becoming traumatized by any potential traumatic experiences. In other words, students are taught to build resiliency before enduring overwhelming psychological stress. Furthermore, Dr. Arasz is a public speaker for various institutions focusing on Control Theory, anxiety, and trauma.

With her revised book, "Why On Earth Do I Feel This Way: Understanding anxiety and mental health through control theory", Dr. Arasz aims to better equip students, parents, schools, and communities, including law enforcement and first responders, to understand the root of mental health more fully by using her clinical theory as the basis of her work while incorporating a more in-depth neurological application to her theory. Dr. Arasz continues to advocate for mental health education in schools of all levels. She is also expanding her work into training law enforcement officers to help them better understand how to process traumatic and stressful events themselves, as well as understand how to respond to/engage with citizens from a neurological perspective with a more comprehensive understanding of trauma on the brain.

Printed in the USA
CPSIA information can be obtained
at www.ICGtesting.com
LVHW062343091023
760591LV00045B/1180/J

9 781957 776781